TOP POCKET

COMPUTER DICTIONARY

A-Z of Microcomputers

D1809615

Longman Top Pocket Series

TOP POCKET

COMPUTER DICTIONARY

A–Z of Microcomputers

Charles J Sippl

Longman Group Limited,
Longman House, Burnt Mill, Harlow,
Essex CM20 2JE, England
and Associated Companies throughout the world.

First published 1984

Sippl, Charles
    Top pocket computer dictionary: the A-Z of
    microcomputers
    1. Microcomputers – Dictionaries
    I. Title
    001.64′04′0321   QA76.5

    ISBN 0-582-55568-X

Computer typeset in Great Britain
by Computerset (MFK) Limited,
Saffron Walden, Essex.

Printed in Great Britain by
Robert Hartnoll Ltd, Bodmin

Editorial: Myles Hewitt, Lesley Wright

Foreword

This handy pocket guide to the language of microcomputers is a must for all who use this modern technology in their daily lives.

For work or play, for adults or children, the *Top Pocket Dictionary of Computers* provides an easy-to-use, ready guide to the A to Z of microcomputers.

Microcomputers —
the background

The development of the microcomputer can be traced back 100 years to when Sir Charles Babbage invented the first computer, although his 'Analytical Engine', as he called it, was never actually built. The first working computer was built in the early 1930s in Germany from parts supplied by the radio industry, its development spurred on by the needs of the rearmament policies leading up to the Second World War. In the USA, similar needs led to the development of the Electronic Numerical Integrator and Computer (ENIAC) which was first used to compute ballistic tables for bombing.

After the war the commercial applications for computers began to be recognized. But the 'first generation' computers cost fortunes to build, they had thousands of parts, used great lengths of cable and filled enormous rooms which needed to be air-conditioned because of the amount of heat they created. They worked by thousands of valves which were unreliable and required the continual presence of skilled engineers.

In response to the commercial demands for computers, the new computer companies such as

IBM put much effort into research and development. In 1948 the transistor was developed which led to the 'second generation' of computers. The transistor made computers smaller, cheaper and more reliable. As the market expanded, prices dropped from millions to hundreds of thousands of pounds.

The major technological revolution, which preceded the microcomputer, came in the 1960s with the advent of the silicon chip. Using silicon technology, it became possible to put a number of transistors on to one silicon wafer. This led to calculators becoming a big consumer product by the late 1960s.

Then, in 1971, a Californian company called Intel designed and launched the first single chip which had enough transistors on it (some 2,000) to make a complete processor in itself – this was called a microprocessor. Since then more and more sophisticated microprocessors have been developed, incorporating larger and larger memory capacities. Refined manufacturing techniques and mass production led to a big reduction in the cost of computing power.

The development of the microprocessor led to the first home computer. This came in the form of a self-build kit from a small American firm called MITS. It was launched onto the American market in January 1975 and cost just 420 dollars. It captured the imagination of hundreds of electronics enthusiasts. By the end of 1976 there were some 30,000 hobby computers around plus 300 computer stores in the USA.

In 1977 Commodore introduced its PET, the first ready-assembled microcomputer with a keyboard, screen and a cassette drive to provide additional memory capacity. It filled the gap between the self-build kits for the hobbyist and the business user without any computer experience who needed more power. Microcomputers have never looked back. Many more companies began to produce microcomputers, including the legendary Apple which was started by two enthusiasts in their garage in California in 1976 and which turned into a multi-million dollar enterprise.

In the UK Sir Clive Sinclair's ZX81, priced at under £50, meant that even children were able to buy a computer which 20 years ago would have cost many thousands of pounds, and which would have filled a major concert hall. It is not surprising that computers are so popular when you can get so much power for so little money. At home, microcomputers can be used to learn how to program, play games, and keep domestic accounts, to teach young children to read and count, and to help older children to revise for examinations.

A simple device called a modem enables home computers to be connected to central, more powerful computers over the telephone line. This enables homes to receive software directly, to pass messages to other users and to receive other information, rather like an 'electronic magazine'. The potential is great. There are already experiments in certain parts of the country for 'teleshopping', whereby people are able to order goods from shops without actually having to go there in person. This service would especially help the old and disabled. The system can be extended to other activities like home banking and even to booking your holidays.

More powerful microcomputers can be used by all sorts of businesses to help reduce tedious, repetitive tasks, and to achieve them hundreds of times more quickly and efficiently. Word processing can be done via the microcomputer; also accounting, draughting, record keeping – the list is endless. Big companies can give individual employees their own microcomputer which can, if desired, be linked to the company's own large mainframe computer from which information can be downloaded.

Computers can help travel agents, for instance, by supplying immediate information about bookings while a customer is present, and further bookings can be made with the push of a button. Estate agents can enter details of houses and can match them up with suitable prospective purchasers. In school, many subjects such as mathematics, geography, history and science are now being taught with the help of microcomputers. The microcomputer can also be used by shops as a cash register and to alert the shopkeeper automatically if stock of a particular product is getting low.

Microcomputers are used extensively by the health services. Many doctors use microcomputers in their surgeries to keep patient lists and records. At the push of a button, a doctor can call up a patient's records on screen and will be able to see immediately if that patient is allergic to any kinds of drug, for instance. Dentists are also beginning to use microcomputers. At each visit the patient's check-up details, treatment and charges can be entered to build up a history which can be easily called up on the screen at any time.

The new, smaller 'portable' computers are also useful. They can be used while the owner is travelling, for example. They can also be very resilient, work in extreme temperatures and can be dropped without any ill-effects. This makes them useful to the military. So soldiers may now use a portable computer instead of pens and clipboards for checking off and making notes on missile systems for maintenance and repair work, even on the battlefield.

In a very short time, microcomputers come to help people in all walks of life. As development continues and the hardware and software become more advanced, so the applications will become more and more sophisticated.

A

A
The digit in the hexadecimal numbering system that corresponds to the decimal value of 10. For example, the decimal number 160 is written in hexadecimal as A0.

abend
The halting of a computer program usually because of a program error or system fault before the job has been completed. Stands for *ab*normal *end*.

absolute address
1 The actual location in storage of a unit of data **2** The character or group of characters indicating location in storage which the central processing unit (CPU) can interpret directly.

absolute value
In mathematics, the absolute value of a number is its positive value.

acceleration time
A measurement of the time passing between the interpretation of a read or write instruction from the CPU to a peripheral device and the actual moment when the data transfer begins. Acceleration time is also called start time.

acceptance test
A test used to demonstrate the capabilities and workability of a new computer system.

access *(verb)*
to ~ information

access
To retrieve information from or store information in a computer memory device.

access time
The amount of time required from the instant that the CPU asks for data from a peripheral storage device until that data is transferred to it.

accounting, message
A system, maintained by a switching device, which records statistical data concerning the messages it handles; e.g., number of messages to and from each station, message lengths, queue lengths, and so on.

accumulator
A special memory location within the CPU used to perform arithmetic operations. Typically data is brought from memory into the accumulator, operated on, and moved back into a memory location.

acknowledgment (ACK)
A character or group of characters generated at a receiving device to indicate to the sending device that information has been received correctly.

acoustic coupler
A device which provides the communication between a remote terminal and the computer by means of a telephone handset and telephone lines. The handset is placed in the acoustic coupler which converts data into a sequence of tones which are then transmitted over telephone lines.

active file
A file for which there are transactions for most of the stored records during each processing cycle.

ADA
A high-level computer programming language designed for real time applications and to control the simultaneous performance of several operations.

ADAPT
A compiler system for the numerical control of tools. Used to produce tapes to drive numerically controlled machine tools.

add time
Time required for a computer to perform an addition, exclusive of time required to obtain quantities from storage and put sum back into storage.

address *(noun)*
Each location in computer memory is identified by an address, which allows the computer to find the location of a specific data item (or instruction).

address *(verb)*
To call up data from or place it into a memory location.

address format
The particular arrangement, layout, or organization of the address portion of a computer instruction.

address modification
An operation which causes an address to be altered.

address, single
A code that specifies a single station that is to receive traffic.

addressability
Addressability refers to the capability of a unit of memory to be addressed.

aggregation
A type of record structuring that physically arranges groups of data items that have been defined by some data model.

ALGOL
A computer language developed by an international committee in the 1960s. ALGOL stands for ALGOrithmic Language.

algorithm
A sequence of instructions that tell how to solve a particular problem.

alignment notches
Two small semicircular notches in the floppy disk jacket which ensure the disk is properly inserted in the disk drive.

alphanumeric
1 A contraction of alphabetic-numeric. **2** Pertaining to a character set that contains both letters and numerals, and usually special characters.

alternative route
See ROUTE, ALTERNATIVE.

AM
See AMPLITUDE MODULATION.

amplification
1 The strengthening of a weak signal. Contrasts with attenuation. **2** The ratio between the output signal power and the input signal power of a device. **3** Gain.

amplitude
The strength of a signal. Amplitude and time are the two parameters of any signal.

amplitude modulation (AM)
A method of conveying information through a carrier signal by modifying the carrier signal's amplitude. The most common use of AM is in radio broadcasting, although it is also used in data communications.

analog

Pertaining to data in the form of continuously variable physical quantities. Contrasts with DIGITAL.

analog computer

A computer that uses physical quantities – such as voltage, current, or resistance – to represent numerical quantities to solve operational problems.

analysis

The study of problems using systematic procedures breaking down the complex entity into constituent parts and examining their relationship, the ultimate goal being the construction of an algorithm for computer solution.

analyst

A person who determines the overall functions to be performed by a computer system and determines the major tasks the system will carry out.

analytical graphics

Business graphics which are intended for use as analytical, decision-making tools as opposed to graphics suitable for presentations to clients.

anti-aliasing

A technique used to increase resolution in computer graphics. Images are filtered so that the edges become blurred. The lack of sharp contrast and softer look gives the appearance of greater resolution.

APL
A programming language created in 1967 to be a highly interactive, conversational language. It has a very comprehensive set of primitive operators which carry out actions requiring dozens of statements in other programming languages.

append
To add something to the end of something else. For example, when data is added to the end of an existing file, the file is said to have been appended.

applications software
The software that performs the specific jobs to be done in a business. For example, programs that perform order entry, accounts payable, accounts receivable, and general ledger. Applications software also refers to any general purpose program for an end user. Good examples are word processing and database programs.

architecture
The interconnection and organization of internal circuitry in a microprocessor or computer.

arithmetic logic unit (ALU)
That part of the CPU which performs arithmetic operations. The ALU is composed of circuitry which is able to do binary arithmetic and Boolean logic operations.

arithmetic relation
A relation which consists of two arithmetic expressions separated by a relational operator, such as $<$, $>$.

array
A data structure containing two or more logically related elements of the same type which are identified by a single name. In general, elements in an array are stored in consecutive locations in the main memory.

artificial intelligence
An area of study in the field of computer science. Artificial intelligence is concerned with the development of computers able to engage in human-like thought processes such as learning, reasoning, and self-correction.

artificial language
A programming language whose rules and syntax were explicitly developed before it was used. For example, PASCAL and COBOL are both artificial languages.

ASCII
American Standard Code for Information Interchange, in which binary numbers represent alphanumeric symbols.

assembler
A program which takes the mnemonic form of the

computer's language and converts it into binary object code for execution.

assembly language
Low-level symbolic language used for writing source programs. The symbolic instructions are translated into machine-language commands before being used by the computer.

associative storage
A memory device in which a location is identified by its contents rather than by names or position.

asynchronous circuit
A circuit without a synchronizing clock pulse whose operation is triggered only by signal levels.

asynchronous computer
One in which each operation starts as a result of a signal generated by the completion of the previous operation or by the availability of the equipment required for the next operation.

asynchronous transmission
Data is transmitted at irregular intervals by placing a start bit before each character and a stop bit after each character.

audit trail
A system for tracing the flow of data through a computer or business system.

autochart
A type of documentor used for the automatic production and maintenance of charts, principally flowcharts.

automatic check
A provision constructed in hardware for verifying the accuracy of information transmitted, manipulated, or stored by any unit or device in a computer.

automatic programming
The process by which a computer automatically translates a 'source' program, in programming language, into an 'object' program, in machine code. This is accomplished by an assembler or compiler loaded into the processor's memory.

auxiliary operation
An operation performed by equipment which is not controlled by the central processing unit.

auxiliary storage
A storage device that is under the control of the computer, but not directly a part of it, e.g., disk and tape.

B

B
1 The abbreviation used in programming languages for 'binary'. In some programming languages,

especially assembly languages, the binary equivalent of the decimal number 10 would be written as 'B1010', or 1010B. **2** The hexadecimal digit that corresponds to the decimal value of 11. For example, the decimal number 176 would be written in hexadecimal as B0.

background program
A program with a relatively low-priority level. Background programs will not be executed until higher-priority programs have finished being executed.

backplane
A printed circuit board (PCB) which contains sockets other PCBs can plug into it at right angles. Generally, a backplane does not contain electronic components.

backspace
To move backwards instead of forwards, as with the print mechanism on a typewriter or printer, or the cursor on a CRT screen. To backspace a file is to move towards the beginning of the data.

band
1 A range of frequencies between two defined limits. **2** A group of recording tracks on a magnetic drum.

band printer
A type of line printer that uses an embossed steel band to form the letters printed on the paper.

bandwidth, nominal
The maximum range of frequencies, including guard bands, assigned to a channel. Only the range between the guard bands is usable for data transmission under most circumstances.

bar printer
An impact printer which prints fully formed characters, one line at a time, by striking type bars against an inked ribbon and paper.

base
The radix of a number system, i.e., the decimal system has a base of ten; the binary system has a base of two.

base address
A given address from which a final address is derived by combination with a relative address.

baseband
1 The frequency band occupied by the aggregate of the transmitted signals before they have modulated a carrier. **2** A signal in the frequency band of (1).

BASIC
One of the easiest computer languages to learn, popular with beginners and small computer users.

batch
A group of all instructions or data relevant to a program or a group of similar programs that is retained in batches for processing in a single run.

baud
A unit of measurement of serial data transmission which is usually taken to represent bits per second.

benchmark
A test that measures the speed, accuracy or other operational parameters of computer equipment. The performance of a computer system is tested by using special programs known as benchmark programs.

benchmarking
A traditional technique for evaluating different computer systems by running the same job on each and comparing the time required for completion.

binary
A number system that uses only two digits: 0 and 1. Binary numbers are well suited for use by computers, since many electrical devices have two distinct states: on and off.

binary arithmetic
The arithmetic of the number system which uses only two digits: 0 and 1.

binary dump
A dump recorded in binary representation, instead of the more commonly used hexadecimal representation.

binary search
A very efficient algorithm for searching for an item in a list of sorted data. The binary search examines the

central item in the file, then the central item of the top or bottom half of the file, continually dividing the file in half until the item is found. This is the most efficient search for use on a file of sorted data.

binary-coded decimal (BCD)
Pertaining to a decimal notation in which the individual decimal digits are each represented by a group of four binary digits.

binding time
Time in which the actual memory address is determined.

bpi
See BITS PER INCH.

bi-stable
The capability of assuming either of two stable states, thus of storing one bit of information.

bit
Short for 'binary digit'. Bits are represented in computers by two-state devices, such as flip-flops or magnetic cores. A bit is the smallest unit of information which can be held on a computer.

bite
See BYTE.

bit rate
The rate at which binary coded signals are transmitted in a specified length of time.

bits per inch
Unit used to measure the recording density of magnetic tape.

bit stream
A string of bits transmitted over a communication line. There are no separations between the groups of characters.

bitmapped graphics
In bitmapped graphics, each pixel on the screen is represented by its own bit in memory. Bitmapped graphics are used to create detailed, high resolution graphics.

black box
1 A general term for describing any type of electronic device built for a special purpose, or which causes a system to function in a non-standard fashion. **2** Any electronic or mechanical device which performs specified functions but whose inner workings are unknown to the user.

blank
A condition usually represented by no perforation in a given character location on a punched tape or card. Sometimes used as a control character.

block
A sequence of characters or bytes which are grouped together to be treated as a complete unit of information. Typically, blocks consist of a fixed number of

bytes, called the block length. Data contained in blocks is used extensively in data communications and when storing information on tape or disk.

block cipher
This cipher method enciphers fixed-sized blocks of bits under the control of a key that is often approximately the same size as the blocks being encoded.

block length
A measure of the length of a block generally expressed by the number of characters within that block. Also called block size.

blow up
A program is said to have blown up if it ends unexpectedly because of a bug or because it encounters data conditions it cannot handle.

bomb
A program is said to have bombed if its output is incorrect or if it cannot execute because of syntax or logical errors.

Boolean algebra
The study of operations carried out on variables that can have only two values: 1 (true) and 0 (false); developed by George Boole, a 19th century mathematician, as principles of mathematical logic.

bps
Bits per second. Used to measure the speed of data transmission.

branch
A path in a program that is selected from two or more paths by a program instruction.

breakpoint
The point in a program at which the program stops running. Breakpoints are set by a programmer to check for errors in the program.

broadband
See wideband.

broadcast *(noun)*
A broadcast is a message transmitted to several or all users of a computer system. For example, the statement 'The system will go down in 5 minutes' would be a broadcast if it was transmitted to the users of the system.

broadcast *(verb)*
To transmit to all stations on a circuit, as opposed to one or a particular group of stations.

B-rules
Rules in a backward production system. They are applied to goal descriptions to produce subgoal descriptions.

bubble memory
A memory system that consists of tiny cylinders of magnetization whose axes are perpendicular to the crystal sheet on which they are located. Bubble memory allows a very high density of data storage.

bubble sort

An algorithm which sorts a list of items into ascending or descending order. A bubble sort works by scanning the list in several passes, and in each pass 'bubbling' the highest number to the top of the list.

bubble sorting

A method of sorting achieved by exchanging pairs of elements.

buffer

A device for the temporary storage of data that is located between two other devices of differing speeds, e.g., output from computer (faster) will be held in a buffer before it is sent to a printer (slower).

bug

A fault or error in a computer program.

bus

An electrical route between several devices along which data flow.

business graphics

Computer graphics images produced to aid businesses in either analysis or presentation of information to clients, especially slides or large transparencies for projection.

byte

The smallest group of bits which can be addressed individually. A byte usually contains eight bits. Each byte corresponds to one character of data, representing a single letter, number, or symbol. The byte is the most common unit of measuring computer storage capacity. See K.

C

C
1 The name of a high-level, problem-oriented programming language. C is a highly structured language that bears a strong resemblance to PASCAL. **2** The digit in the hexadecimal numbering system that corresponds to the decimal value of 12. For example, the decimal number 192 is written in hexadecimal as C0.

CAD/CAM
Abbreviation for computer-aided design/computer-aided manufacturing; this refers to graphics software developed to assist in design and manufacturing.

calculator mode
An operating mode, available with some computer systems, which allows the terminal to be used as a desk calculator.

call-directing code (CDC)
A two- or three-character code used in teletypewriter systems to activate a particular machine or group of machines.

capacitor
A device for storing an electric charge on two conducting plates separated by an insulating material.

capacity
The amount of information that all or part of a computer can store. For example, a 48K computer will have a main memory capacity of 48 Kilobytes of data.

capacity, circuit
1 The number of communications channels that can be derived from a given circuit at the same time. **2** The information capacity, measured in bits per second, of a circuit.

card reader
Unit that converts the data coded on punched cards into an electronic form acceptable for entry into a primary storage unit. Card readers were common input devices at one time, but are now obsolescent.

carriage return
In a character-by-character printing mechanism, the operation that causes the next character to be printed at the left margin.

carrier transmission
See TRANSMISSION, CARRIER.

CCD
See charge-coupled device.

central processing unit
See CPU.

channel
A part of the computer that connects it with its peripheral devices. All communications between the computer and its peripherals pass through a channel.

channel, digital
A channel capable of carrying direct current, as opposed to analog channels, which do not.

channel, grade of
Refers to the relative bandwidth of a channel: narrowband, voiceband, wideband.

channel type
See TYPE, CHANNEL.

character
Any symbol that can be stored and processed by a computer.

character, check
A parity character added to a group of characters to assist in error detection-correction.

character, control
1 A character whose occurrence in a particular context initiates, modifies, or stops a control operation or function. 2 A character used to initiate functions such as line feed, carriage return, etc.

character generator
A chip which stores the pixel patterns the computer uses to display the character set onto the screen.

character printer
Character printers print one character at a time, unlike line printers which produce an entire line print in one operation. Character printers are slower than line printers but can offer better quality printing.

character reader
A device capable of locating, identifying, and translating into machine code, hand-written or printed data appearing on a source document.

character recognition
The technology of using a machine to sense, and encode into a machine language, characters which are written or printed to be read by human beings.

character set
See SET, CHARACTER.

character, special
In a character set, a character that is neither a numeral nor a letter.

characters per second
Abbreviation cps. This is the term used to describe the speed of operation of a character printer.

charge-coupled device (CCD)
A special type of computer memory chip offering high storage density with low power consumption.

check character
See character, check

check, cyclic
A method of error detection which checks every nth bit, n + 1 bit, n + 2 bit, and so forth.

checkpoint
A place in a routine where a check, or a recording of data for restart purposes, is performed.

chip
A small integrated circuit package containing many logic elements; a small piece of silicon impregnated with impurities in a pattern to form transistors, diodes, and resistors.

cipher
An algorithmic transformation performed on a symbol-by-symbol basis on any data.

circuit
Complete path for an electric current.

circuit card
A printed-circuit board containing electronic components.

circuit capacity
See capacity, circuit.

circuit, four-wire
A system in which the transmitting and receiving paths are separate channels.

circuit, integrated
See INTEGRATED CIRCUIT.

circuit switching
The ability to establish a direct connection between points or between two or more network ports. This can consist of either a direct electrical connection or a direct logic path through gates.

circuit, two-wire
A system in which all transmitting and receiving is performed over one pair of wires (or equivalent).

cladding
The transparent medium which surrounds the core of an optic fibre.

clear
To erase the contents of a storage device by replacing the contents with blanks or zeros.

clock
A circuit that generates a series of evenly spaced pulses. A computer with a faster clock rate is able to perform more operations per second.

clogged ink-jet nozzles
A problem created when the ink in an ink-jet printer

comes into contact with air and dries, collecting inside and around the nozzle, jamming the system.

closed

1 A switch is closed when it is turned on, allowing current to flow through it. **2** A file is closed when data cannot be read into it or written from it.

COBOL

Common Business Oriented Language. Most widely used programming language in large commercial data processing systems.

CODASYL

Conference on Data Systems Languages. An organization for computer users.

code

1 The particular form in which information is entered into a computer (e.g., binary, ASCII, hexadecimal). **2** Code is often used to refer to the instructions contained in a computer program. For example, 'How many lines of code does your program contain?'.

code, binary

Any code using only two distinguishable code elements or states, representing the binary digits 1 and 0.

code conversion

A procedure for changing the bit grouping of a character in one code into the corresponding bit grouping in a different code, such as a change from EBCDIC code to ASCII code.

code, machine
See MACHINE CODE.

code, morse
A system of dot-dash signals for communications. Not used for data communications.

coder
Slang term for programmer.

coding
Coding is the process of writing program instructions.

coding errors
Errors caused by the programmer writing the instruction incorrectly.

coldstart
A method of resetting the computer. The contents of memory are erased and the computer is started up again 'cold'.

collate
To merge two or more ordered sets of data or cards in order to produce one or more ordered sets which still reflect the original ordering relations.

collating sequence
The sequence formed by characters in a particular coding system. Usually special characters are lower

in value than alphabetic which are in turn lower than
numeric.

collator

A device used to collate or merge sets or decks of
cards or other units into a sequence.

colour hard copy device

Any peripheral output device that provides the user
with hard copies (charts, graphs, drawings, or text)
in multiple colours. These devices include pen plotters, electrostatic, impact, and ink jet printers, and
almost any normal hard copy device with the incor-
poration of additional colours.

column

A vertical arrangement of characters, bits, or other
expressions. Contrasts with row.

column, comment

Usually column 1 on punched cards which is reserved
for comments.

command

An instruction to a program or software system telling it to perform some action or to cause the
execution of a certain program. For example, a print
command causes the contents of a file to be printed.

comment

A statement in a computer program that is not acted
on by the computer, but that gives information to
clarify the purpose of a set of instructions. Informa-

tive comments can be extremely valuable if, for example, another programmer has to amend the program at a later date.

communication channel
A path used for transmission of data.

communication link
Consists of the hardware and software used to provide the means for two devices, such as a computer and a terminal, to be connected so they can transmit data.

communications
The means of conveying information of any kind from one person or place to another.

Communications Satellite Corporation (COMSAT)
A privately owned company, chartered by the U.S. Congress for voice and television signal communication by satellite.

compaction
The process of rearranging data on a disk so as to clear large areas of free storage space. As data is constantly being written and erased from a disk, especially during heavy processing, it tends to get scattered (fragmented) into small portions called extents. As this occurs, the search, retrieval, and storage processes are slowed down, which reduces the overall efficiency of the program. Frequently, a

special compaction routine resolves this by locating, reassembling, and consolidating the fragmented extents. Compacting is also referred to as compressing.

compatible
Two devices are compatible if they can work together without special hardware or software having to be used to make this possible.

compile
To produce a machine-language routine from a routine written in high-level language.

compiler
A computer program that takes as input a program written in a high-level programming language and puts it into a form known as machine language which can be understood and acted on by the computer.

compress
To condense data, with any of a variety of methods, so that it occupies less storage space.

computer
Any device capable of accepting information, applying prescribed processes to the information, and supplying the results of these processes.

computer graphics
The processing and generation of visual information using a computer linked to a keyboard and CRT.

computer output microfilm (COM)
Film produced by converting computer-generated signals into readable characters at high speeds. A small piece of film can contain many pages of information in a reduced form. This can be magnified and read using a device known as a COM reader.

computer family
A group of all the models of a certain type of computer. Computers in a computer family share the same logical design.

computer literacy
Knowledge of computers and how to use them to solve problems.

computer science
Computer science is a cognitive science. It is concerned with the design and application of computer hardware and computer software.

computer-aided design (CAD)
The use of a computer-based system to assist in the design of electronic circuits, machine parts for industry, and so on.

COMSAT
See COMMUNICATIONS SATELLITE CORPORATION.

concatenate
To combine two or more items, end to end, to form a larger item. For example, concatenating the string

'time' to the string 'wise' produces the string 'timewise'.

concentrator
A type of multiplexer.

condition
In the COBOL system, one of a set of specified values that a data item can assume.

conditional branch
A branch that only occurs if a certain condition is met.

conductor
A material in which electric current can flow easily. In order for a material to be a conductor the electrons must not be too tightly bound to their atoms.

configuration
Refers to the way in which a computer and peripheral equipment are connected and programmed to operate as a system.

conjunction
Conjunction is the name given to the AND operation. A conjunction is true only if its propositions are all true.

connect time
The time interval from the initial connection to the final breaking of a communication.

console
A device, such as a control panel, that allows people to communicate directly with a computer.

constant
A value written into a program instruction. The value does not change during the execution of the program.

constraint
In mathematical programming, an equation or an inequality specified in a problem. This creates restrictions which limit the solution to the optimal one.

contact pair
See CROSSPOINT.

contamination
The storage of data in the wrong place in the memory, and thus destroying important data, or even the program itself. In most cases, if the program does not abend, further processing will result in unpredictable output. Contaminate is loosely synonymous with corrupt.

contiguous
Storage locations are said to be contiguous if they are adjacent to each other.

continuous forms
Forms fed into a printer on a continuous roll. Continuous forms are perforated at regular intervals so

that they may be separated after printing has been completed.

control character
See CHARACTER, CONTROL.

CONTROL key
A key on the keyboard whose effect is similar to the SHIFT key in that it does nothing unless it is pressed while another key is being pressed. The effect of both keys being pressed is to generate a nongraphic character which is recognized by the computer as a control code, which initiates a function of the computer or one of its peripherals.

control panel
A control panel is part of an operator console. The control panel contains light indicators, switches, and buttons which are used to turn the power on and off, to control the computer system's various components, and to monitor the computer's activities.

control section
The portion of the central processing unit which directs the step-by-step operation of the entire computing system.

control sequence
The sequence in which a program's instructions are executed. The instructions are executed one at a time and in order from first to last until a branch instruc-

tion transfers control to another portion of the program.

control signals
Electrical signals which go to and come from the control unit in the central processing unit. These control signals direct the computer to perform a sequence of operations.

control unit
The part of the central processing unit (CPU) responsible for receiving instructions from a program in main memory, decoding them, and sending control signals to appropriate units in the computer in order to execute them. The control unit is a controller which directs the operation of the computer as a whole.

conversational language
A programming language that uses a near English character set which facilitates communication between the user and the computer.

conversational mode
Communication between a terminal and a computer in which each entry from one elicits a response from the other, maintaining real-time man-machine communications.

copy
The process of transferring information from one location to another.

core
Small iron rings (less than 1 millimeter in diameter) that were formerly the main components of computer memory. Now antiquated.

corrupt
To change or destroy information so that its validity is questionable.

counter
A device such as a register or computer storage location used to represent the number of occurrences of an event.

coupling
The process of connecting two systems together so that they can communicate with each other. See acoustic coupler.

CP/M
Control Program for Microcomputers is the most popular operating system for small computers. CP/M commands are used to keep track of the data and programs stored on disks, and to determine the programming language being used.

cps
1 Characters per second. **2** Cycles per second. Now referred to as hertz (Hz).

CPU (Central Processing Unit)
The main part of a computer system where arithmetic and logical operations are performed. It also

contains the main memory and carries out system control functions.

crash
To become inoperable. Computer systems crash when there is a malfunction in the equipment. Programs crash when they contain an error.

cross-assembler
An assembler that translates a program into a form that can be run on a different computer than the one on which the cross assembler runs.

crosspoint
An electronic circuit that can electrically connect or disconnect two conductors in response to some external control signal. Synonymous with contact pair.

CRT (Cathode Ray Tube)
A device whereby electrons are sprayed onto a viewing screen under the direction of magnetic fields to form patterns. CRT is often used as a synonym for visual display screen.

crunching
A way of condensing programs to pack the most instructions into the smallest space. By crunching a program, it uses less memory space and runs more efficiently.

cryogenics
That branch of physics which studies the use of

devices that utilize the properties assumed by materials at temperatures near absolute zero.

current
A flow of electrons through a conductor.

cursor
The small 'blip' of light that traverses the CRT screen indicating where the next character typed will appear. Usually a cursor is a square or rectangle the size of a character, or a dash the width of a character, and in many cases it flashes off and on to draw the operator's attention to it.

cursor arrows
The keys on a keyboard that are marked with arrows, and control the movement of the cursor without explicitly typing characters. The direction of the arrows on the keys indicate in which direction the cursor will move.

customer engineer
See FIELD ENGINEER.

cut off
The point of degradation at which a signal becomes useless due to attenuation and/or distortion.

cybernation
The use of computers coupled with automatic machinery to control and carry out complex operations.

cybernetics
The study of control theory and communication between and among people and machines.

cycle stealing
Cycle stealing is the taking of an occasional machine
cycle from a CPU's regular activities in order to
control such things as an input or output operation.

cycle time
See MACHINE CYCLE.

cyclic check
See CHECK, CYCLIC.

D

D
The digit in the hexadecimal numbering system that
corresponds to the decimal value of 13. For example,
the decimal number 208 is written in hexadecimal as
D0.

daisy-wheel printer
One of the main types of impact printer. Daisy-wheel
printers print fully formed characters, one at a time,
by rotating a circular print element composed of a
series of individual spokes, each containing two
characters, that radiate out from a center hub. Daisy-
wheel printers are often used with word processors.

data
Data is factual information. 'Data' is the plural of the word 'datum', which means 'a single fact'. Data processing is the act of using data for making calculations or decisions. Strictly speaking 'data' is a plural noun, but in practice it is almost invariably used in the singular. For example: 'After the data has been input…'. A computer uses various types of data, such as words and numbers.

data adapter
The data adapter is a special processor which converts the input data or output information to or from the internal codes used by the computer.

data aggregate
A collection of data items, units of named data, within a record given a name and referred to as a whole. For example a data aggregate called DATE could be composed of data items called MONTH, DAY, and YEAR.

database
A collection of data arranged in files used for more than one purpose.

database management system (DBMS)
A software package used to keep track of a database. The system must be able to locate particular items in the database, to add new data or change old data when needed, and be flexible so that people with different needs can have access to the database.

data bus
One of three buses which make up a system bus. A data bus transfers words in the computer from one location to another. For example, a data bus is responsible for transferring words from the central processing unit (CPU) to main memory.

data cell
A mass storage device which utilizes strips of magnetic tape housed in a rotating cylinder.

data check
An error in the data read, caused by a flaw on the recording surface of a magnetic tape or disk or other such medium. This type of error cannot be corrected at that place nor can that particular portion of the recording surface be used again.

data compression
The elimination of all blanks, unnecessary fields, and redundant data from various records, in order to reduce the amount of storage space needed to contain them.

data element
A combination of one or more data items that forms a unit or piece of information.

data item
A data item is the smallest unit of named data and may consist of any number of bits or bytes. Data items are often called fields or data elements.

data management (DM)
A general collective term referring to the functions of a system which provide access to data, enforce storage conventions and regulate the use of input/output devices.

data medium
The material or mode in or on which data is represented.

data preparation
Organization and storage of information in a form that can be input into the computer.

data processing
The operations performed on data to achieve a desired objective.

data pulse
An electronic signal sent by the disk-drive head to create a tiny magnetic field on a disk.

data reduction
The transformation of raw data into a more useful or condensed form.

data set
An IBM term which means 'file'. More specifically, a data set is a set of data that is recognized and accessed as a unit. See also FILE.

data set organization (DSORG)
An IBM term meaning the same as 'file organiza-

tion'. More specifically, it is the general structure of a data set or file (sequential, direct, partitioned, and so on).

data transfer rate
The rate at which data is read or written from or to the disk. The higher the transfer rate, the quicker the data is fed into the system and the more efficient it is.

data type
Refers to the various kinds of information the computer can store. For example, different data types include alphanumeric or character data, decimal numbers and integers.

datamation
A contraction of 'data automation', which refers to automatic data processing.

dataphone
A trade mark of the AT&T company to identify the data sets it manufactures and supplies for use in the transmission of data over the telephone network.

deadlock
A state of affairs in which two or more processes are waiting for events that will never occur.

debug
To locate and correct errors and their sources in a computer program, either manually or through the use of special debugging routines.

debugging

1 The process of isolating and removing bugs from computer programs. **2** The process of determining the correctness of a computer routine and correcting any errors.

decimal

The number system with a base of ten.

decimal-to-binary conversion

The process of converting a numeral written to the base ten to the equivalent numeral written to the base two.

decimal table

A listing of all the contingencies to be considered in the description of a program, together with the corresponding actions to be taken.

declaration, procedure

The act of naming and writing a procedure. Some programming languages require that a procedure be declared, that is, given a formal name along with its code, so that it can be called later, by using its name in lieu of an instruction.

decode

To determine the meaning of individual characters or groups of characters in a message through the reversal of some previous coding.

decoder
A circuit which translates data from one coded form to another, or interprets a specific code.

dedicated
A communications line or other device such as a printer used for a specific purpose only.

default
The assumption that will be made by a program if a contradicting statement is not made by the programmer. In other words, a variable will take in a default value unless a different value is specifically assigned to it.

delay
The difference in time between a cause and its effect, such as the transmission and receipt of a pulse.

delimiter
A delimiter is a character responsible for separating units of information, such as strings of characters.

demodulation
The process of retrieving intelligence (data) from a modulated carrier wave, the reverse of modulation.

dense list
A dense list is a list that fills up all the available storage space. A record cannot be added to a dense list until either more storage space is allocated to the list or until a record is deleted from the list.

densitometer
An optical-electronic device that measures the degree of darkness of photographic images.

density
The amount of binary information that can be stored per unit area on a magnetic storage medium such as tape or disk.

device driver
A software package that controls the timing and operation of external devices.

diagnostic
Refers to a message generated by a compiler or interpreter to assist in program error correction.

diagnostic message
A message the computer prints in case of an error to help the programmer or engineer identify the cause of the error.

diagnostic routine
A routine used to locate a malfunction in a computer or to aid in locating mistakes in a computer program. In general, it is any routine specifically designed to aid in debugging or trouble shooting.

dial-up
The use of a dial or pushbutton telephone to initiate a telephone connection between a terminal and a computer.

digit

A symbol representing a positive integer in a given numbering system. For example, a bit is a binary digit representing 0 or 1 in the binary number system. Also, the numbers 0 to 9 are all digits in the decimal number system.

digit, check

A redundant digit (or digits) carried within a unit item of information (character, word, block, and so on) which provides information about the other digits in the unit in such a manner that an error can be spotted.

digital

1 Data in discrete quantities. Contrasts with ANALOG. **2** Pertaining to data in the form of digits.

digital channel

See CHANNEL, DIGITAL.

digital-tape cassettes

These cassettes consist of cartridge-enclosed, magnetically-coated tape to record and play back text. Information on a cassette is accessed serially.

digitize

To convert an analog measurement of a physical variable into a number expressed in digital form.

digitizer

Any device that can convert analog measurements

into digital quantities for digital computer processing.

diode
A device used to permit current flow in one direction in a circuit and to inhibit current flow in the other.

direct address
One which specifies the exact storage location of an operand.

direct addressing
An instruction addressing mode in which the memory reference specifies a memory location that contains the data to be operated on.

direct file
A method of file organization in which records are stored sequentially but, unlike a sequential file, each record is of a fixed length. Fixing the length of the records allows the retrieval time to be reduced.

direct memory access
A procedure used to transfer data between a computer and a high speed storage device without using the CPU.

direct video storage tube (DVST)
A CRT which holds a constant image. DVSTs have very high resolution and picture quality and are used in computer-aided design.

direct-access storage device (DASD)
A direct-access storage device is a device with each physical record having both a discrete location and a unique address.

directory
A file containing the names, sizes, locations, and other relevant information about all the files contained on a disk.

disk
A computer memory device which looks something like an audio record. It is either hard or floppy. See FLOPPY DISK, HARD DISK, MAGNETIC DISK.

disk controller
A printed circuit card that contains the integrated circuit (IC) chip necessary to activate and control a computer's disk drive.

disk drive
An electromechanical device into which a disk is inserted to read or write information.

disk drive controller
A hardware interface between the disk drive and the computer, which controls the operation of the disk drive.

disk drive head
An electromagnetic device which sends and receives data pulses allowing it to create magnetic fields on a

disk or read information already stored in magnetic
fields on the disk.

diskette
See FLOPPY DISK.

disk operating system (DOS)
An operating system on disk backing storage.

disk pack
A number of magnetic disks connected by a central
spindle and enclosed in a protective package.

disk reader
A device that converts information stored on disks
into signals that can be sent to a computer.

disk storage unit
A random-access data storage device which gives
rapid access to data.

dismount
To remove a magnetic storage medium from its read/
write device. For example, one can dismount a magnetic tape from its tape drive.

dismountable pack
A floppy disk or other storage medium that can be
dismounted from its read/write device and replaced
by another. Dismountable packs contrast with nondismountable packs, such as fixed disks.

display
The visual representation of information on a CRT or other display device.

distributed data processing (DDP)
Data processing in which two or more connected computers share the work load.

divider
The device or unit that performs division for the computer.

documentation
Descriptions that accompany a computer program to explain to people how the program works.

dog
The word form of the digit in the hexadecimal numbering system that corresponds to the decimal value of 13. It is written as 'D'.

dot-matrix printer
A printing device that forms each character from rows and columns of dots. A matrix is an array of items organized into rows and columns. For example, a 5 x 7 printer forms characters 5 dots wide and 7 dots high.

double density
Twice the amount of binary information that can be stored per unit area as compared to the standard density for that particular medium. Double density usually applies to floppy disks.

double precision
Precision obtained by coupling two computer words to represent one number in fixed-word-length computers.

double word
Multiple adjacent bytes beginning on a double work boundary, that can be handled as a single unit.

down
A computer system is down when it is not available to users for some reason.

down-line
See DOWNLOAD.

download
To transfer a copy of a program, file, or other information from a remote database or other computer to the user's own terminal over a communications line. Download is synonymous with down-line loading.

downtime
The period of time during which a computer system is down, or not operating. Downtime usually refers to the operating time lost due to an error or malfunction.

drum
A computer storage device in which data items are stored on rotating metal cylinders.

drum printer

An impact printer which prints a line of fully formed characters by striking an inked ribbon and paper against a rapidly rotating drum. The drum contains a complete set of embossed characters that circle it at each print position, forming a row of As, Bs, Cs, Ds, etc, across its surface. As the drum rotates, all the As in a line are printed, all the Bs in the line are printed, and so on, until the drum has made a complete revolution.

DSORG

See DATA SET ORGanization.

dual intensity

A method whereby some characters are displayed on a monitor more brightly than others, under the control of the program displaying the characters. In simple terms, this method allows certain data to be emphasized.

dual-port RAM

See SHARED MEMORY.

dummy

An artificial element in a program used only to fulfill specifications in the program and not to actually perform a function. Examples of dummy items are dummy variables, dummy instructions, dummy addresses and dummy blocks.

dummy variable
A dummy variable or dummy argument is a variable that is used as a spaceholder and type specifier in the definitions of subprograms. Dummy variables inform the computer how many arguments the subprogram will take, and specify the data type of these arguments. When a subprogram is called, the dummy arguments are replaced by the actual arguments used in the calling statement.

dump *(noun)*
A list of the contents of a computer's main memory.

dump *(verb)*
To copy the contents of all or part of memory, usually from an internal storage device into an external storage device.

duplex transmission
A method of transmission whereby data can be transmitted and received simultaneously. Often referred to as full-duplex, to emphasize the difference from half-duplex.

dyadic
See BINARY.

dynamic programming
A mathematical procedure for optimization of a multistage problem solution used in operations research and systems analysis.

dynamic RAM

A class of random access memory that requires periodic servicing (a refresh cycle) in order for the contents to remain valid.

dynamic storage allocation

A method of making storage capacity available to programs and data based on actual, immediate needs.

E

E

The digit in the hexadecimal numbering system that corresponds to the decimal value of 14. For example, the decimal number 224 is written in hexadecimal as E0.

EBCDIC (Extended Binary Coded Decimal Interchange Code)

A computer code in which a character is represented by a particular pattern of eight binary digits.

edge detection

An algorithm by use of which a computer or robot may understand what objects it 'sees'. After the optical sensors input a picture of one or more objects, the algorithm attempts to differentiate between one object and another object, shadow, and background, by finding all of an object's edges and comparing the object's outline with objects stored in memory.

edit
To rearrange data or information. Editing may involve the deletion of unwanted data, the selection of pertinent data, the application of format techniques, the insertion of symbols, and the testing of data for reasonableness and proper range.

effective throughput
The average throughput of a data-processing device. Effective throughput is contrasted with rated throughput and provides a more accurate measurement of the efficiency of the device than its rated throughput.

effective address
The address of the memory location that is actually accessed during execution of an instruction that requires memory access.

electron
A subatomic particle with a negative electric charge.

electronic components
These are wires, transistors, diodes, resistors, capacitors, inductors, and so on.

electronic office
An office which uses electronic equipment, such as computers, word processors, etc, to process, store and deliver information.

electrostatic printer
A high-speed printer that uses charged pins to form character matrices on chemically treated paper.

electrothermal printer
A high-speed printer that uses heated elements to create characters as matrices of small dots on heat-sensitive paper.

elegant
A program is elegant if it uses the smallest amount of main memory possible. Thus, an elegant program contains no statements which are not essential.

encode
to translate data into a particular code.

encryption algorithm
Any algorithm that implements a cipher.

end of file
A mark at the end of a data file.

enter
This is a key on a computer terminal which is pressed at the end of each line in order to enter the contents of that line into the computer. Also called return key.

entry point
The address of the first instruction executed in a computer program or in a section of one, such as a routine or subroutine.

environment
A computer system's environment consists of those operating conditions under which it was designed to operate.

error message
A brief message displayed to the user when the program in execution encounters an abnormal situation or an error in the data. The error message contains a brief explanation about the nature of the error.

ESI control
Acronym for Externally Specified Index control. A type of buffer control which makes it possible to handle a number of computer channels. ESI allows other transactions to run without interruption.

ETX
Abbreviation for End-of-TeXt. It is a control character used to designate the end of text in a message or text file. In ASCII, the ETX character is represented by the ASCII code '003'.

even parity
See PARITY, EVEN.

executable form
A program written or translated into machine language, which is ready for the computer to execute.

execute
To execute an instruction is to do what the instruction says to do.

executive routine
A routine which controls loading and relocation of routines and in some cases makes use of instructions which are unknown to the general programmer.

expandable
A computer is expandable if it can have more memory added to it or if it can have more disk drives added to it, additions that will expand the computer's storage capacity. Most home computers are expandable.

expansion
The process of extending a data structure from a compressed state to its normal state for printing. For example, a string of characters that stores consecutive spaces with two bytes will be expanded.

expansion board
A printed circuit board (PCB) that adds additional capabilities and functions to a computer's hardware. The expansion board plugs into a slot inside the computer, and is generally accessed by referencing the address assigned to the slot.

expression
A series of symbols which forms a unit to which meaning is assigned.

extent
A collection of physical records, continuous in secondary storage. The number of records in an extent

depends on both the physical size of the volume and the user's request for space allocation.

external sort
A sorting algorithm which sorts data contained in secondary storage, such as a magnetic tape or disk storage unit.

external sorting
The sorting of data which is located in an external storage device, such as a disk unit. External sorting is used for large groups of data which will not fit completely in the computer's memory all at once.

F

F
The digit in the hexadecimal numbering system that corresponds to the decimal value of 15. For example, the decimal number 240 is written in hexadecimal as F0.

fan-in
The number of devices that can be connected to an input terminal of a circuit without impairing its function.

farad
The unit of measure of capacitance.

fatal error
Any error during the execution of a program that causes the program's execution to halt.

feed holes
Holes along the sides of computer printer paper that allow the paper to be driven by a sprocket wheel.

feedback
It occurs when a control device uses information about the current state of the system to determine the next control action.

fibre-optic cable
A bundle of thin, coated-glass rods. Light introduced into one end of a rod travels the rod's length, emerging at the other end. Variations in light intensity travelling through a fibre-optic rod relay information in the same way as variations in electrical current travelling through a wire.

field
A group of adjacent characters is called a field. See DATA ELEMENT.

field engineer
A field engineer is a person who repairs computer equipment. Field engineers usually work for computer vendors or computer repair services and are often called FEs or CEs (customer engineers).

FIFO
See FIRST-IN-FIRST-OUT.

file

A file is a collection of information stored as records. Files are stored on peripheral memory devices, such as a disk memory or a tape memory.

file compatibility

If files are compatible, it means that data-file disks for a particular program can be moved between two computers. This is one of the main criteria in assessing the compatibility between two microcomputers.

file organization

This is the general structure of files for a given application. Generally, there are four different types of file organization, each of which has its own advantages and disadvantages. These are, in order of increasing complexity: sequential, direct, indexed sequential, and partitioned. Usually, file organization is considered on the level of program development, so that each program uses the one file organization (or more than one) that best suits its intended application.

file protect ring

A file protect ring is a plastic ring that must be in place on the back of a magnetic tape in order for data to be written on the tape. Thus, when the file protect ring is not in place, the data is protected against accidental or unauthorized writing.

filler

One or more non-data characters placed in a field so

that all the positions in the field are occupied. Fillers are used to bring fields to a standard size.

filling
See PADDING.

firmware
This refers to the computer programs encoded permanently into ROM. These programs are referred to as microprograms, and cannot be altered or erased. Common examples of firmware are microcomputer operating systems and video game cartridges.

First-In-First-Out (FIFO)
This is a technique of storing and retrieving data in certain data structures. The most common data structure that uses the FIFO method is the queue. In FIFO, the first data item stored in the queue is the first one to be retrieved. Thus, a data item stored in the queue must wait until all data items 'in line' ahead of it are retrieved before it can be retrieved. FIFO is contrasted with LIFO See LAST-IN-FIRST-OUT.

fixed
Something is said to be fixed if it is not allowed to change. For example, a fixed disk is a disk that is permanently mounted on a disk drive.

fixed point
A numeration system in which the bit position of one

decimal is fixed with respect to one end of the numerals.

fixed word-length computer
A computer in which all machine words are of the same length. The registers and storage locations in this type of computer are designed to contain the number of bits contained in each machine word.

fixed-length record
A fixed-length record always contains the same number of characters.

flag
1 This is a symbol that marks some computer output messages, such as error messages, to indicate that they deserve special attention. **2** Any of various types of indicators used for identification, such as word mark; or a character that signals the occurrence of some condition, such as the end of a word.

flip-flop
A type of electronic circuit which can assume one of two states. Flip-flops are used as memory elements, and state changes are produced by electrical signals.

flippy disk
A floppy disk that records data on both sides.

floating point arithmetic
This uses a variable location for the decimal point in each number.

floppy disk

A disk made of some nonrigid material upon which data can be stored.

flowchart *noun*

A pictorial representation of an algorithm used in a computer program. Flowcharts are composed of symbols that represent the different types of operations – for example, a diamond represents a decision, and a parallelogram represents an in-put statement. The completed flowchart depicts graphically the overall logic and flow of control that is used in the program.

flowchart *verb*

To describe and document the individual steps in a process.

flowline

A line linking two flowchart symbols. The flowline has an arrowhead to represent the direction data transfer or program control proceeds.

FM

See FREQUENCY MODULATION.

forbidden

This refers to an illegal character or operation.

format

Format is a term used to refer to the specific arrangement and location of information within a larger unit of storage.

FORTRAN

This is the most widely used scientific computer programming language. FORTRAN stands for FORmula TRANslation language. It was developed for IBM computers in the late 1950s.

fourth generation computer

A modern digital computer that uses large-scale integration circuitry.

fox

The word form of the digit in the hexadecimal numbering system that corresponds to the decimal value of 15. It is written as 'F'.

fragmentation

This is the phenomenon that occurs on disks (and other storage devices) most often during processing that requires frequent updating of files. The continuous process of storing and erasing data on a disk tends to break up files into small pieces, called extents, which become scattered over the disk. This leads to an ever decreasing efficiency in the search-retrieval and storage algorithms in the program. Because of this loss of efficiency due to fragmentation, special compaction algorithms are needed to periodically find and regroup a file's extents.

frame

A vertical strip on magnetic or paper tape on which a single character, or byte, can be stored.

freeware
Software which a seller gives to a user free cf charge.

frequency
The measurement of the number of cycles of an audible tone or alternating current per second. One cycle per second is known as a Hertz, abbreviated Hz.

frequency division multiplexing (FDM)
The use of an electrical path to carry two or more signals at different frequencies. One computer-related example is the full-duplex modem, which carries signals to and from terminals.

frequency modulation (FM)
A means of conveying information by modifying the frequency of a carrier signal. The most common use of FM is in radio broadcasting, although it is also used in data communications.

full-duplex
See DUPLEX TRANSMISSION.

full-screen terminal
This allows the operator to type in characters anywhere on the display screen. By way of contrast, a line-at-a-time terminal allows the operator to type only at the bottom line of the display.

function
A set of instructions that takes one or more numbers

and then performs some operation on them to yield a single value.

functional unit
A unit in a computer system capable of performing arithmetic, storage, control, input, or output functions.

G

garbage
This general term refers to faulty data, acquired noise from a communications line, incorrect commands, any other useless or undesirable input, or data already in the computer which is no longer needed.

garbage collection
A procedure that makes more memory available by locating those storage units in main memory that contain data no longer needed by the current program.

garbage in, garbage out (GIGO)
GIGO is a term meaning that if a program is given bad data (garbage) for input, it will produce bad results (garbage) for output.

gate
A circuit that contains one or more input signals and produces a single output depending on its function.

gather-write
Refers to placing information from non-adjacent locations in memory into a physical record such as a tape block. Opposite of scatter-read.

GIGO
See GARBAGE IN, GARBAGE OUT.

glitch
A small bug that causes an error in data transmission. Glitches are usually caused by electrical noise or by a voltage surge.

global knowledge
In artificial intelligence, global knowledge is the knowledge of a problem's complete solution. It is responsible for telling the control system which rules or pieces of knowledge are applicable to the problem.

global variable
A variable with a name that has the same meaning throughout all the subroutines of a program.

go to sleep
A slang term that is used when a computer program either halts or appears to do nothing because it is trapped in an infinite loop. For example: 'The system went to sleep because my program had an endless loop in it.'

GOTO-less programming
A slang term for structured programming, so named

by the fact that it discourages the use of the GOTO statement.

GOTO statement
An instruction in a high-level language.

graph, acyclic
A graph with no cycles. Acyclic graphs are also loop-free and simple.

graph, complete
A graph in which any two distinct nodes are adjacent. Thus, every node is adjacent to every other node.

graphic display
A computer terminal that displays information, such as drawings and pictures, on a screen, usually a cathode ray tube, TV terminal, or video terminal.

graphics
The field in which computers are used to manipulate data in the form of pictures.

guard bands
Bands which protect the head carriage from the sudden jarring of the disk drive assembly against the chassis at the limits of carriage movement.

guest operating system
In a piggyback operating system mode, the guest operating system is the operating system that is being simulated by the 'host' operating system.

H

half adder
A computer circuit capable of adding two binary digits.

half-duplex transmission
Mode of transmission used for communication which is capable of sending and receiving data in both directions, but not simultaneously. During transmission, one modem is the transmitter and the other modem is the receiver.

halt
To terminate the execution of a program via an instruction, error, or interrupt.

handler
A routine that either handles input/output operations or controls the operation of an input/output device.

handshaking
The exchange of predetermined signals when a connection is established between two communicating devices.

hanging
A condition in which the computer will not respond to input, because it is unable to escape from a loop, attempting to execute an illegal or non-existent in-

struction, or trying to access a non-existent peripheral device. Hanging of the system usually results in the computer continuously repeating the instructions which caused it to hang. Sometimes referred to as hang-up.

hanging prevention
Computer logic which prevents any set of legal or illegal instructions from hanging the system.

hang-up
See HANGING.

hard copy
A printout on paper of computer output.

hard disk
A storage device made of ceramic or aluminium using a single disk or a stack of several disks.

hard failure
Failure of a device or component that cannot be resolved without first repairing the device. For example, a sudden power surge may be enough to burn out a chip, causing a hard failure and requiring repair of the equipment.

hardware
Consists of all the physical elements in the computer, such as integrated circuits, wires, and keyboard.

hardware configuration
The arrangements, relationships, and general archi-

tecture of the various devices (disk drives, printers, modems, and so on) that make up a computer system. Hardware configuration also includes all physical and electrical paths which connect these devices.

hash
Useless information present within a storage medium. Hash can be data that is no longer being used, or serves as a 'filler' for fixed-length blocks of data. Hash is synonymous with garbage.

hash total
The addition of all of a specific field in a group of records which, when compared to a previous hash total, can help ensure that all the records are present.

head
A device incorporating a small electromagnet that reads, records, or erases data on a storage medium, such as a magnetic disk or tape.

head access window
An oblong slot in the floppy disk jacket which allows the disk-drive head access to the information stored magnetically on the disk.

head crash
A physical collision which occurs when a read/write head touches the surface of a disk.

head-load control
The electrical method used to load heads to the medium before reading or writing.

Hertz (Hz)
This is a measurement of the frequency of an audible tone or alternating current. One Hertz is equal to one complete cycle per second, and is abbreviated as Hz.

heuristic
A method used when there are several approaches to a solution, but no one approach is known to solve a problem consistently. This method examines the problem and then tries an approach that seems most appropriate in solving the problem at hand. A solution is found by trial and error.

hexadecimal
Number system based on 16 digits 0–9, A, B, C, D, E, F, designating 16 different possible values.

high resolution bit mapped display
A display technique which uses a single memory location within the computer to control a particular dot of light on the screen, thus significantly increas-. ing the clarity and definition of graphic images on the screen.

high-level language
A computer programming language designed to allow people to write programs without having to

understand the inner workings of the computer. High-level languages do not translate from one high-level instruction to one machine instruction. It is not unusual for one high-level instruction to translate to a dozen machine-code instructions.

high-order bit
The left-most bit in a word.

holography
A method of recording images on a film without a lens.

horizontal tab
A machine function that causes the print mechanism or cursor to move to a specific column while staying on the same line.

host operating system
In a piggyback operating system mode, the host operating system is that which the computer hardware traditionally uses and which runs as one of its tasks a 'guest' operating system.

housekeeping operation
A general term for the operation which must be performed for a machine run, usually before actual processing begins.

hypertape drive
A device which uses magnetic tape cartridges to read or record information at 340,000 alphanumeric characters per second.

Hz
See HERTZ.

IC
See INTEGRATED CIRCUIT.

icon
1 A pictorial symbol displayed on a user's output device during the execution of a program which is used to give information to the user as a supplement to or in place of verbal information. Icons are often found in educational or computer graphics creation software. **2** A picture used to represent a menu option in a graphics based menu. A menu option is selected by positioning the cursor over the icon which represents the desired option.

image processing
Computer enhancement of photographs to increase clarity and detail.

immediate addressing
An instruction addressing mode in which the memory reference specifies not a memory address but the actual data to be operated on.

impact printer
A printer which operates by striking individual raised characters or wire ends against an inked rib-

bon and paper. Impact printers print either fully-formed characters or dot-matrix characters at a rate of one character at a time or one line at a time. The seven main types of impact printers are: bar printers, chain printers, drum printers, wire-matrix printers, train printers, thimble printers, and daisy-wheel printers.

inches per second
Measurement of the speed at which a pen plotter produces a hard copy.

index
1 The subscript of an array of data which denotes a specific item in the array. For example, SALES(5) would show the fifth entry of an array called SALES. **2** A value used inside an index register which provides for indexed addressing.

index register
A register within a computer's CPU, decremented each time through a loop that uses the index registered. For example, an index register may be used within a loop to access consecutive locations in memory, such as arrays, or to serve as a counter to monitor the number of times the loop should be performed.

index addressing
A mode of addressing in which the effective address is found by adding the contents of an index register to the given memory reference.

indexed array
An array of data items in which the individual items can be accessed by use of a subscript or index. An indexed array is also called a subscripted array, subscripted list, or indexed list.

indexed list
See INDEXED ARRAY.

indexed sequential access method (ISAM)
An access method in which indices, which can be used to provide direct access to a file that would otherwise only provide sequential access, are stored with sequential files. The index, for each file, contains keys for every record in the file as well as their corresponding location, such as the track number on a disk.

indexed sequential file
A method of file organization in which each record has a variable length and is stored sequentially, similar to a sequential file. Unlike a sequential file, however, the indexed sequential file reserves a portion of memory to serve as an index to the locations of all records in the file. Thus, only a small amount of memory is used for nonusable data, and the index serves to lessen the average retrieval time of a particular file.

indexing
The method of address modification used to access data in an array or table.

indirect addressing
An instruction addressing mode in which the memory reference specifies a memory location whose contents are another address.

information
Information is data previously processed by a computer and produced as meaningful output.

information hiding
A software design concept the purpose of which is to reduce interaction between sections of a program.

information processing
The manipulation of data so that new data appears in a useful form.

information retrieval
See RETRIEVAL, INFORMATION.

information science
The study of the creation, manipulation and communication of information in all its forms.

information system
The network of all communication methods within an organization

initialization
The act of setting variable information – such as storage locations, counters, and variables – to starting values. Initialization of variables is usually the first step in a computer program.

initialize
To preset a variable or counter to its proper starting values before commencing a calculation.

ink-jet printer
A printer which forms characters by spraying a fine jet of precisely directed ink onto the paper. It is almost silent in operation.

ink plotter
A device which outputs pictures and text from a computer onto paper by means of one or more ink pens in holders whose movements are controlled by the computer.

input *(noun)*
The input to a computer is the data or programs fed into the computer for it to process. The data or programs may be entered into the computer via a keyboard, magnetic tape, disk, and so on.

input *(verb)*
To enter data into a computer or data-processing system.

input-bound
A device is said to be input-bound if it can output data at a faster rate than data is being input to it. For example, a computer using paper-tape input is input-bound.

inquiry
A technique by which the interrogation of the con-

tents of a computer's storage may be initiated at a keyboard.

instruction pipeline
The instruction pipeline is the direct information channel through which machine instructions pass from macro to micro level.

instruction register
A register within the central processing unit which stores a copy of the instruction currently being executed.

integer
A number in the set of all positive and negative whole numbers. 18, −43, and 0 are all examples of integers. However 18.76, −43.93, and 0.32 are not integers.

integrated circuit (IC)
An electronic device consisting of many miniature transistors and other circuit elements on a single silicon chip. An important type of integrated circuit is the microprocessor.

interactive
An interactive computer system is a system in which the user communicates with the computer through a terminal, and the computer presents the results immediately after an instruction has been entered.

interactive compiler
A compiler that translates each statement entered on

a terminal into machine language as soon as it is entered.

interactive graphics
Graphics in which the user interacts with the graphics display to control the content of the display. Examples include computer simulations and computer-aided design.

interactive processing
A mode of processing in which the computer is updated almost instantaneously. There is generally some form of dialogue between the system and its operators.

interblock gap
A gap on tape or disk which separates blocks or physical records.

interface
A boundary point at which different elements of the system are linked together or between a human and a computer system. For instance, the interface between the user and the system might be the VDU keyboard.

interference
Noise or some other disturbance in data transmission which may result in errors or in the loss of data.

interlaced scan
A scanning system used for raster graphics and CRTs in which the even numbered lines are scanned alter-

nately with the odd numbered lines, instead of sequentially.

interleaving

The mixing of actual data with control information when transmitting data on a communications path. Control information includes identically spaced check characters to assist the computer in detecting data transmission errors. The receiving terminal must be able to interpret the interleaved information according to set rules and formats, so that if it finds an error it can signal the sending terminal to retransmit the block of data.

intermittent error

An error which occurs at random. This type of error is usually caused by an external condition, such as dust on a recording medium's surface, and may disappear when the recording medium (disk or tape) is moved.

internal sort

A sorting algorithm that sorts data which is contained entirely within the computer's memory. This contrasts with an external sort which sorts data in secondary storage. Internal sorts are used on small files where all the data can be contained within memory at one time.

Internal Telecommunications Union (ITU)

A 156 member specialized agency of the United Nations responsible for the international coordination of matters related to telecommunications, including telephone, telegraph, radio, and TV.

interpreter
A program which translates a high level source code into machine language. Unlike a compiler, which produces an object program to be run later, the machine language produced by an interpreter is executed immediately.

interrecord gap
The space between records on a magnetic tape.

interrupt
To stop running program in such a way that it can be resumed at a later time, meanwhile permitting some other action to be performed.

interrupt service routine
A routine used for handling the condition causing an interrupt. For example, if a program was interrupted due to a lack of memory, the interrupt service routine would allocate more memory, and return control back to the program.

intrinsic function
A standard function built into a computer language.

inversion
The process of reversing the state of binary digits by changing the magnetization of each bit.

I/O
Abbreviation for input/output. Input is data and instructions entered into a computer, perhaps via a keyboard or magnetic tape. Output is all information received from the system, perhaps as hard copy printout or as a display on the screen.

iteration
An iteration is one pass through a sequence of computer program instructions. Several passes through the same sequence of instructions, such as in a loop, are called reiterations.

iterative process
Any process that requires more than one repetition (iteration) of the same procedure or set of instructions. A loop is one such example of an iterative process in computer programming.

ITU
Abbreviation for International Telecommunications Union.

J

job
A specified group of tasks prescribed as a unit of work for a computer. By extension, a job usually includes all necessary computer programs, linkages, files, and instructions to the operating system.

joystick

An input device which consists of an upright lever mounted in a ball and socket joint together with an activating button. When a joystick is used in conjunction with an output display screen, the lever can be tilted in any direction in order to move a cursor in a corresponding direction on the screen. The activating button is used to perform a desired action at a specific cursor position, such as selecting an item from a menu or drawing a point at the cursor position.

joystick, absolute

A joystick which provides a one-to-one correspondence between all of its various positions and all the points on the display screen with which it is used.

joystick, rate

A joystick which moves a cursor at a fixed rate over a display screen in a direction corresponding to the direction of the joystick handle. This kind of joystick is good for making slow, precise movements of the cursor.

jump

Refers to the process by which a computer interrupts its normal sequence of processing instructions in a program and abruptly starts processing from a different location in the program. Jumps are also referred to as branches.

K

K

The letter 'K' represents the number 2^{10} or 1024. Also, the letter K is usually used in the expression representing a computer's capacity. For example, a personal computer's capacity, the number of bytes in its main memory, might be expressed as 64K (65,536 bytes). K is also used loosely to mean 1000.

kernel

Allocator and manager of memory in an operating system. It shares CPU time among programs, coordinates inter-program signals and accepts and hands out jobs to appropriate I/O chips.

keylock

A lock on a terminal which prevents it from being used unless a key is in the lock and turned to the 'on' position. Keylocks are useful in preventing the use of a terminal by unauthorized persons.

keypunch *(noun)*

A machine that punches holes in cards according to a machine-readable pattern. The machine is now old fashioned.

keypunch *(verb)*

To punch holes in cards according to a machine-readable pattern.

keypunching

Refers to the method which was once the main way of preparing data for mainframe computers. Keypunching requires specially trained operators who enter data into cardboard cards, using special machines that punch rectangular holes. The process is now old fashioned.

keyword-in-context index (KWIC)

An index which lists titles alphabetically according to their keywords. There is an entry for each keyword in the title. An index of this type is prepared by highlighting each keyword of the title and aligning the keywords in a vertical column alphabetically.

kilobyte

See K.

kludge

A slang term that refers to a make-shift hardware and/or software system. A kludge is made from various mismatched parts and is consequently both temporary and rather unreliable.

L

label

1 A name, in a program, that identifies an instruction, a data value, a file, a record, a device, or a storage location. **2** A marker used to designate the location in a PASCAL program to which a GOTO statement will cause a jump to occur.

label record
A record on a file of magnetic tape that contains identifying information about that file.

language processor
A program which translates symbolic instructions to machine code. There are three types of language processors: assemblers, compilers, and interpreters.

language subset
A part of a language that can be used independently of the remainder of the language.

language translator
An assembler, compiler, or other routine that accepts statements in one language and produces equivalent statements in another.

large scale integration (LSI)
LSI refers to the process of putting large numbers of transistors and components on a very small chip thereby reducing the size of main memory storage.

laser memory
A mass storage device on which information is stored and read by a laser.

laser printer
A non-impact printer which uses laser beams to form dot-matrix characters on a photoconductor. The

characters are then transferred to paper, one page at a time.

Last-In-First-Out (LIFO)

A technique for storing and retrieving data in certain data structures. The most common data structure that uses the LIFO technique is the stack. In LIFO, the last data item stored in the data structure is the first to be retrieved. A close analogy is a stack of plates, in which the last one placed on the stack must first be removed before any of the subsequent plates can be removed.

latency time

The time interval between the read/write head of a disk drive arriving at the proper track just as the proper sector has passed by, and when the beginning of the sector passes beneath the head.

leading zeros

Zeros appearing to the left of a number in a storage location. For example, the number '00843' has 2 leading zeros and the number '000943' has 3 leading zeros.

LCD

See LIQUID CRYSTAL DISPLAY.

LED

Abbreviation for Light Emitting Diode. An LED device will light up when the proper current is passed through it.

LEFT$

The LEFT$ function in BASIC selects a specified number of characters from the left edge of a specified string variable. Thus LEFT$(A$, N) will select the first N characters of the string A$.

legal

Something is legal if it is acceptable to a computer system's software rules. This includes syntax rules. If a statement or word in a program is not legal, then the program will not run. Instead, it will produce an error message.

letter quality

A letter-quality printer uses type elements of sufficiently high quality that the output looks as though it came from a typewriter.

LF

See LINE FEED.

librarian

A person who has responsibility for safekeeping of all computer files, such as programs and data files on magnetic tapes, disk packs, microfilm, punched cards, and so on.

library

The area on a magnetic disk that is used to hold programs.

LIFO

See LAST-IN-FIRST-OUT.

light emitting diode
See LED.

light pen
A small pen-like input device used with a CRT to make a selection from a list of choices, create a drawing on the CRT, and so on.

line feed (LF)
The control character used to advance the paper in a printer or the cursor on a screen to the next line. In ASCII, the LF character is represented by the ASCII code '010'.

line printer
A printer that produces a line at a time as opposed to a character printer, which prints a single character at a time.

linkage editor
A linkage editor is a device to combine into a single module a set of program instructions that have been independently compiled.

linked list
A data structure in which each item in the list is composed of two elements: the information itself, and a pointer to the next element in the list. The advantages of linked lists are that new elements are created as they are needed and that items can be easily added to or deleted from the list. For instance, to add an element to an ordered list it is necessary

only to change two pointers rather than resorting the entire list.

liquid crystal display (LCD)
A type of video display that consists of a sandwich of two glass sheets, spaced approximately .0005 inches apart and sealed at the perimeters. Between the two plates flows a liquid crystal solution.

liquid crystal display, colour-pigmented
A display that uses liquid crystal solutions that appear as colours other than black when electrically excited.

liquid crystal (LC) bar-graph panel indicator
A type of bar-graph indicator that uses a series of liquid crystal segments to provide image. Other bar-graph indicator technologies use light-emitting diodes, electroluminescence, and gas-discharge.

LISP
A computer programming language whose basic data structure is a binary tree.

list, linear
A linear list is a list with no sublists, where a sublist is a list within a larger list.

list structure
A list containing one or more sublists, where a sublist is a list within a larger list. For example the list *(a, b, c, (aa, bb))* is a list structure because the last item in the list *(aa, bb)* is a sublist.

literals
Any data or messages to be output exactly as they are indicated in the instruction.

LOAD
A command that causes information to be transferred from a peripheral storage device to the computer's main memory.

load point
A light-reflective marker indicating the beginning of the usable portion of a magnetic tape. When a tape is rewound it is returned to this point.

load-and-go
An operating technique which achieves rapid response and simple operation because no delays or stops occur between the loading and execution phases of a program.

loader
A program which loads another program into memory. Loaders are often used on programs which are ready to be run.

local terminal
A computer terminal located at the same site as the central computer. Local terminals can therefore be directly connected to the central computer.

logic device
A device which performs a logical operation in a

computer. Gates, combinational circuits, and sequential circuits are all examples of logic devices.

logic error
An error in a program caused by faulty reasoning of the programmer.

logic gate
An electronic switching component which accepts one or more values as input, evaluates them, and produces one output value according to a specific logical operation.

log-off
To enter into a computer the information needed to end a session on a terminal.

loop
A set of statements in a computer program that are to be executed repeatedly.

low-level languages
Symbolic programming languages that are coded at the same level of detail as machine code and can be translated in a ratio of one symbolic instruction to one machine-code instruction.

LSI
See LARGE SCALE INTEGRATION.

M

machine code

The fundamental language of the computer. It is written as strings of binary 1s and 0s. Each machine code instruction tells the central unit of the Central Processing Unit (CPU) what to do.

machine cycle

The amount of time necessary for the computer to perform one operation. Machine cycle is also called cycle time.

machine-dependent

A machine-dependent program works on only one particular type of computer.

machine error

A deviation from correctness due to equipment failure.

machine-independent

A machine-independent program can be used on many different types of computers.

machine instruction

An instruction written in machine language. Machine instructions can be read and directly executed by the computer. However, because they are composed only of 1s and 0s they are extremely difficult for a person to read and understand.

machine language
The binary code which a computer can immediately understand. All high level languages must be translated into machine language before the commands can be executed by the computer.

machine-readable
Data is machine-readable if it has been recorded in such a way that it can be read or sensed directly by the computer. For example, data recorded on tape is machine-readable.

macroinstruction
An instruction consisting of a sequence of microinstructions which are inserted into the object routine for performing a specific operation. A macroinstruction usually combines several operations in one instruction.

magnetic core
A tiny piece of magnetic material capable of storing one binary digit. Made of such materials as iron, iron oxide or ferrite and in such shapes as wires, tapes, doughnut-shape solids, or thin film, it was formerly used in making main memory for computers, but is not used in modern machines.

magnetic disk
A flat, circular plate with a magnetic surface on which data can be stored by selective magnetization of portions of the flat surface. May be made of rigid material (hard disk) or flexible plastic (floppy disk).

magnetic drum

A peripheral storage device consisting of a cylinder with a magnetic surface on which data can be stored by selective magnetization of portions of the curved surface.

magnetic tape

A plastic tape with a magnetic surface on which data can be stored by selective polarization of portions of the surface. Often referred to as 'mag tape' or merely 'tape'.

magnetic-ink character recognition

A form of input for an electronic data-processing system using special characters printed with ink which can be magnetized. Magnetic-ink characters read and transmit the data electronically to a conventional storage device, such as magnetic tape.

magnetic tape unit

A type of secondary storage unit. Magnetic tape units are low in cost but are accessed sequentially which gives slow data-access time.

mainframe

A mainframe computer is a large computer. ·Its capacity is much greater than that of a minicomputer or microcomputer.

malfunction *(noun)*

A failure in a portion of the computer's hardware, causing it to operate incorrectly. When there is a malfunction in a computer system, the computer stops operating and the system is said to be 'down'.

malfunction *(verb)*
To operate incorrectly.

mark sensing
To mark cards or pages with a soft pencil to be read directly into the computer via a special reader.

marker
A symbol on a magnetic tape, placed for sensing to indicate beginning or end of a file or piece of information.

master file
A file that contains records that are to be preserved.

master/slave manipulator
A robotic shoulder, arm, and hand that is guided by a human operator from some distance away.

material dispersion
The spreading of a light pulse inside an optic fibre due to the different wavelengths of light emitted by a source. Because different light wavelengths travel at varying speeds through a material, material dispersion occurs when the light source, such as a light-emitting diode (LED), emits a wide interval of bandwidth.

mathematical programming
The series of techniques used in operations research

to find an optimum solution to linear or nonlinear functions. The optimum solution is found by calculating either the maximum or the minimum value of the function, subject to certain restrictions.

matrix
A lattice-work of input and output leads with logic elements connected at some of their intersections.

mechanical resolution
Refers to the shortest line a pen plotter is mechanically capable of drawing. This is contrasted with addressable resolution, which is the shortest line a user can command the plotter to draw. Mechanical resolution should be as high as, and preferably higher than, addressable resolution. Otherwise the plotter would be accepting commands that it is incapable of performing.

medium
The physical substance upon which data is recorded.

member
A file which acts as a record to a partitioned file. Each member has an individual name, and can be altered in any way without affecting the other members of the partitioned file.

memory
The part of the computer where data and instructions are stored.

memory-addressing mode

The way in which an instruction can address memory – that is, call up or place data into a memory location. The different addressing modes include direct, indirect, immediate, relative and indexed.

memory dump

A printout or screen display of the contents of the memory.

memory-mapped video

The mapping of a screen to an area in memory. Screen display is determined by what is in the corresponding screen memory location.

menu

A list of options which is displayed on a monitor screen during a computer program and from which the user of that program must make a choice. The result of an initial choice is often, but not always, another menu of options.

menu-driven program

A computer program is menu-driven if its various parts are accessed through choices made from menus which are arranged in a definite hierarchy.

merge

A merge describes combining two or more sets of records with similarly ordered sets into one set that is arranged in the same order.

merge sort
A procedure for sorting two or more sets of records in order.

message
In data communications, a message is an item of data with a specific meaning transmitted over communication lines. A message is composed of a header, the information to be conveyed, and an end-of-message indicator.

message retrieval
See RETRIEVAL, MESSAGE.

meta-knowledge
A non-symbolic awareness of how to approach and organize an unfamiliar problem so that both heuristic and factual knowledge is effectively applied.

microcomputer
A computer whose processing unit is based on a microprocessor chip. Microcomputers have an increasing variety of applications in the home, office and many other areas. They are smaller than minicomputers and mainframe computers.

microfiche
A unit of film that is divided into rectangles each typically representing a page of information. The average microfiche contains about 250 pages of information.

microfloppy disk
A 3in, 3¼in or 3½in disk similar to the 5¼in floppy disk.

microfloppy disk drive
A data storage device similar to a floppy disk drive except that it uses 'microfloppy' disks.

microinstruction
A small short command such as 'add' or 'delete'.

microprocessor
This is the chip which is at the heart of a microcomputer, in effect providing the CPU of the system. The term is *not* synonymous with microcomputer which refers to the bigger system built around the microprocessor chip. Microprocessors are also used for control purposes on other machines such as cars and domestic and industrial equipment.

microprogram
Programs that are stored in ROM. A microprogram is permanently burned into ROM and is unalterable. Examples of microprograms are video game programs, and BASIC interpreters.

microprogrammed
A computer is microprogrammed if its control unit within the central processing unit (CPU) activates its circuits through microinstructions stored in the control memory, instead of through permanently wired circuitry.

microswitch
A type of pressure-sensing device that a robot uses to detect the presence of some obstacle by impact. The device consists of a tiny switch which is installed on a robot's arm or body. When the robot bumps into something, the switch is tripped and sends a signal to the robot's processor.

millisecond
Abbreviation msec. A millisecond is .001 (one thousandth) of a second.

minicomputer
A small digital computer which is larger than a microcomputer and smaller than a mainframe computer.

mirror writing/shadow reading
The host computer treats two physical disks as a single logical unit and writes data on both. Reading on one or the other is done according to their respective angular positions, to shorten access time. This technique improves data reliability.

mistake
Use of faulty logic or faulty syntax in program.

mixed mode expression
An arithmetic expression within a program that contains operands of different types. For example, a statement might contain both real and integer type variables.

mnemonic

Symbolic name used for various operations and instructions and used to reference a particular register, certain memory locations, fields, files, and subroutines in a program.

modal dispersion

A form of pulse spreading caused by the different path lengths of light rays entering a core (fibre optic cable) of uniform optical density at different angles.

modelling

The process of representing an object system or idea in some form other than that of the entity itself.

modem

A device which alters data in digital form into wave form suitable for transmission over telephone lines and which carries out the reverse process when receiving data. Stands for *mod*ulator/*dem*odulator.

module

A module is any independent unit which is part of a larger system. Microcomputer systems may be made from several modules.

monadic

See UNARY.

monitor

The screen of a cathode ray tube (CRT). Monitors are usually used with microcomputers. Consequently, people who buy a home computer, or personal computer, may buy a monitor to go with it. With most home computers the domestic television set can be used as the monitor.

Monte Carlo
A type of simulation method that uses random numbers to determine the evolution of a system.

mother board
The main printed circuit board (PCB) in a computer. Other printed circuit boards plug into the mother board so that power and electronic signals can be conducted among the boards.

mouse
A hand-held object with rollers on its base used to control the cursor position on the screen. The mouse is rolled across a flat surface and this produces a corresponding movement in the cursor on the screen.

move
To copy data from one storage location in main memory to another.

multiplex
The act of combining input signals from many sources onto a single communications path, or the use of a single path to transmit signals from several sources.

multiplexer
A device that receives input signals from various

sources and combines them into a single transmission, sending the signals out over one line. The multiplexer receiving the signals then reverses the process by separating the signal components from the stream and redistributing them to their respective destinations.

N

NAK
See NEGATIVE ACKNOWLEDGEMENT.

nanosecond
One thousand millionth of a second.

natural language processing
The capability of a computer to understand everyday language, such as English.

negative acknowledgement (NAK)
The control character that the receiving terminal of a data transmission sends to the transmitting terminal to indicate that a transmission error occurred in the last data block sent. The transmitting end then resends the data block to correct the error. In ASCII, the NAK character is represented by the ASCII Code '021'.

NEW
A command in BASIC that clears the memory and allows the operator to start typing a new program.

network

A system in which terminals and computers are linked together according to such factors as the distance between them, the amount of message traffic expected between them, and the existence of appropriate communications facilities needed to connect them. In some networks there are alternate paths (communication links) from every computer or terminal to every other.

nibble

Half a byte. More specifically, a nibble is a string of 4 bits seen as a unit.

node

Any terminal, station, or communications computer in a computer network.

noise

1 Any disturbance which would tend to interfere with the normal operation of a device or system. **2** Spurious signals which can introduce errors in the transmission of data.

nominal bandwidth

See BANDWIDTH, NOMINAL.

nondeletable

Refers to a message or portion of the screen that scrolls off the top of the screen, but can be called to be redisplayed by a specific command.

nondestructive read
A reading process that does not erase the data in memory.

nondismountable pack
A pack (disk or other storage medium) that cannot be removed from its read/write device. Generally, nondismountable packs refer to hard, fixed disks.

nonscrollable
Refers to a line or portion of the CRT screen that does not scroll off the top as new information is written at the bottom. When a nonscrollable message reaches the top of the screen, it stays there, while subsequent messages continue to scroll underneath it.

number cruncher
Number cruncher is the name given to a large computer specifically designed to perform a large number of scientific calculations. A number cruncher's arithmetic-logic unit (ALU) is capable of performing up to 12 million arithmetic operations per second.

numerical control
The control of machine tools or drafting machines through servomechanisms and control circuitry.

O

object language
The output after a translation process. Usually object language and 'machine language' are the same.

object module
The output of a compiler or assembler which contains a program module in instruction form and also control information to guide the linkage editor.

object program
A program that has been translated into machine language and is ready to be run.

octal
A numbering system that uses the base, or radix, of eight. The symbols used in the octal system are the digits 0, 1, 2, 3, 4, 5, 6, and 7. The octal numbering system was widely used in earlier computers, but is seldom used in computers today.

offline
Something not directly connected to the computer, and, therefore, not under the control of the central processing unit (CPU). For example, a keypunch is not directly connected to a computer and is therefore off-line.

online
Refers to a procedure which is under the direct con-

trol of the central processing unit (CPU). This condition usually allows data to be processed immediately, as opposed to batch processing.

online storage
Secondary storage devices that are under direct control of the central processing unit (CPU) such that data is available immediately when required.

op code
The part of an instruction that indicates to the computing equipment what function to perform.

open
1 A file is open when it is ready to have data transferred into it or out of it. **2** A switch is open when it is turned off.

open loop
An information system that makes no provision for automatic error correction or data modification. Such a system requires the operator to make any necessary modification or adjustments.

open-ended system
A system which permits new programs, instructions, subroutines, modifications, terms, or classifications to be added without disturbing the original system.

operand
The item on which an operation is performed.

operating system
A collection of routines, usually software or firmware, used in overseeing the input, and output processing, of a computer program. The tasks of an operating system include: compilation, interpretation, debugging, input/output, garbage collection, memory allotment, and file management.

operation
A defined action. The action specified by a single computer instruction.

operations research
The study of how to do very complicated mathematical operations as efficiently as possible.

operator
An operator is someone who controls a computer or a computer-related device.

optical character reader
A device that can read information directly from a sheet of paper by sensing the locations of the marks in the paper.

optical character recognition (OCR)
The reading of information directly from paper using optical character readers.

optical mark reader
An input device able to read and interpret marks on special input documents.

optic fibre

Optic fibre consists of a core surrounded by a cladding of lower optical density. Light entering the core at a sufficiently shallow angle with respect to the core axis will be reflected back into the core, travelling through the core until it emerges at the other end.

optimize

To get the best possible solution to a problem. This solution is obtained by removing inefficiencies and unnecessary instructions to make the program as short and as fast as possible.

optimized code

A computer program's compiled code that contains no inefficiencies or unnecessary instructions. Optimized code is the best solution to a problem.

optimum coding

The coding of a routine or program for maximum efficiency with regard to a particular aspect, such as reducing either retrieval time or execution, depending on the priority.

output

Data which has been processed and is then made available to the user, perhaps through a printer or display screen, or put onto tape or disk for storage.

output-bound

A device is said to be output-bound if it outputs data at a slower rate than data is being input to it. For

example, a computer that is attached to a slow printer is output-bound if data can be entered at a faster
rate.

overflow
1 An error condition that arises when the result of a
calculation is a number too big to be represented on
the computer. **2** The portion of the result of an
operation that exceeds the capacity of the intended
unit of storage.

overflow check
A test done by the computer to determine whether or
not an overflow has occurred. If the overflow check
reveals that an overflow has indeed occurred, an
error message will be printed.

overflow flag bit
A flag set when an arithmetic result is too large to be
held in memory.

overhead
Overhead is the amount of processing required to
finish a certain task.

overrun error
An error occurring when a transmitted character
arrives at its destination before the previously
transmitted character has been read. When an over-
run error occurs, an error signal is generated so that
the previous character will be retransmitted.

P

pack *(noun)*

1 A magnetic disk or assembly of such disks. **2** A deck of punched cards.

pack *(verb)*

To compress data so that it requires less space in memory or other storage media.

package

A self-contained collection of programs designed to serve some specific set of requirements. Good commercial examples would be the SPSS statistics package that is sold as a unit, word processing packages, and financial single programs.

packed decimal

A packed decimal is a decimal stored in a packed format in order to save storage space and reduce handling overhead.

packet switching

In data communications, packet switching is a method of sending data from one computer or terminal to another. In this method, data is sent in packets of fixed length with each packet being sent separately.

padding

The process of inserting meaningless information,

such as null characters, zeros, or spaces, into the unused portions of fields, records, or fixed-length blocks of data. For example, if a fixed-length block of data is expected to be 128 bytes long, and only 100 are used, the other 28 bytes would be padded with zeros, spaces, or null characters. Padding is also known as filling.

page
A block or unit of fixed length of memory. In microcomputers a page is commonly 256 bytes.

page boundary
The point where one logical page of memory ends and the next logical page begins.

page density
It is the percentage of a page that is covered by text. An average page has about 40 per cent of its page devoted to text. The rest is empty space.

page printer
A printer that produces a page at a time as opposed to a character or a line at a time.

pagination
The process of breaking up a printed report into units corresponding to pages.

paging
In a virtual storage system, paging refers to the swapping of data and programs back and forth from real storage to virtual storage.

parallel cells
Cells are said to be parallel if data can be read from more than one cell at the same time.

parallel run
A technique for converting from one system to another in which the old system and the new system are both run for a period of time until the new system is proven and accepted. Then the old system is discontinued.

parameter
A variable that is held constant during a particular application.

parity bit
A bit that is appended to a byte in order to make the total number of bits either even (even parity) or odd (odd parity).

parity, even
A type of parity checking in which the parity bit's value is set to make the total number of on bits in the byte even.

parity, odd
A type of parity checking in which the parity bit's value is set to make the total number of on bits in the byte odd.

partitioned data set
An IBM term for partitioned file. See PARTITIONED FILE.

partitioned file
A method of file organization in which the file is divided (partitioned) into portions called 'members', each of which is itself a file. The partitioned file has a directory that displays the names, locations, and other relevant information about the files. Partitioned files are less often used for data storage than for storage of related programs.

partitioning
A fixed method of allocating available memory in which each computer device is given its own permanently allocated portion of the computer's memory.

PASCAL
A computer language that is a generalization of ALGOL. PASCAL allows for many different types of data.

password
A secret group of characters that a user must input to log-on to a computer system. This prevents unauthorized persons from obtaining access to the computer or to specific information.

PCB
See PRINTED CIRCUIT BOARD.

PEEK
A command on many computers that allows you to find out the contents of a specified location in the computer's memory.

pen plotter

A hardcopy output device that uses ink pens to provide high-resolution hard copies. Although pen plotters can be slow and require a high degree of user interaction, they provide draughtsman-quality graphics, low initial cost, wide selection of paper size, and extremely low cost per copy.

pen speed

The maximum speed the pen in a pen plotter can achieve. Pen speed is measured in inches per second (ips) and, for small plotters, varies between 12 and 20 ips; large format plotters achieve approximately 35 ips.

peripheral equipment

Any unit of equipment, distinct from the central processing unit (CPU), which may provide the system with outside communication or storage.

peripherals

The mechanical and electrical devices, other than the computer itself, found in a computer system. Peripherals include terminals, tape units, disk units, and printers.

permanent error

An error that cannot be corrected. Such errors usually cause the program to stop prematurely. An example of a permanent error is a data check.

personal computer
A microcomputer used, for example, in a home or office to perform a wide variety of tasks including game playing, word processing, control functions, and business calculations.

personal computing
The use of a computer (usually a microcomputer) by individuals for applications such as business calculations, word processing, and entertainment.

phase jitter
Brief, unwanted distortions in a communications signal. When the duration of such distortions is long enough, or if they are numerous enough, phase jitter can cause loss of information.

phase shift
See SHIFT, PHASE.

photoconductor
Material which varies its electrical conductivity under the influence of light.

Pick
A machine-independent operating system named after its developer, Dick Pick.

picosecond
One-trillionth of a second.

piggyback
An operating system that runs as a task of another,

different operating system. This enables a program to be run on a computer system whose operating system is other than that which the program was written for.

pitch

A measure of the horizontal density of letters, i.e., 10 pitch indicates there are 10 characters per inch.

pixel

An element of resolution on a screen. A pixel or 'picture element' is the smallest portion of the screen which the computer can address as an individual unit.

PL/1

A programming language that has the capacity both to solve complicated numerical problems and to manipulate complicated data files.

plasma panel display

A flat display device composed of tiny neon bulbs. It is used as an alternative to the CRT for graphics displays.

platen

The platen is the part of the printer, either a plate or a cylinder, responsible for supporting the paper on which information is printed.

plotter

A computer-controlled graphics-output device that

moves pens on paper to successive x-y coordinates to make a hard copy of graphics.

plotter repeatability
Plotter repeatability refers to the precision with which a pen can return to a given point. Repeatability is measured in fractions of a millimeter, and it determines how well lines will meet and circles will close.

plugboard
A panel containing a rectangular array of holes into which plugs are inserted to control the operation of equipment. Wires with a plug at each end are connected from hole to hole to form circuits.

POKE
A command on many computers that allows you to store a particular quantity in a specified location of the computer's memory.

polling
A technique by which each of the terminals sharing a communications line is periodically interrogated to determine whether it has some data to transmit or to locate a free channel.

pop
To remove an item from the top of a stack. When an item is removed from the top of the stack it can be thought of as moving every other item up one position.

port
An output in a processor where a peripheral or communications link plugs in.

portable
1 Describes software which can be executed on many different types of computers without major conversion problems. 2 Refers to small, lightweight computers which can be easily moved and used in different locations.

portable computer
A microcomputer that can be taken almost anywhere because it is small, light-weight, and powered by a rechargeable battery pack and/or an AC adapter cord.

portable program
A program that is machine-independent, i.e. which can be used on more than one type of machine.

postprocessor
A program responsible for performing various final operations on data already processed. For example, a postprocessor prepares data for printing.

power supply
Power supply refers to the circuitry within a hardware unit responsible for converting electrical power into the voltages required for the unit's electronics.

precedence rules
That part of a programming language that deter-

mines in what order the computer will perform the operations if a single expression contains more than one operation.

precision
The accuracy to which a quantity is correctly represented or expressed.

predefined process symbol
A flowcharting symbol used to represent a subroutine.

preprocessor
A program responsible for preparing data for further processing. For example, preprocessors may arrange data into different formats, organize it into groups, and perform similar operations on it.

pressure transducer
A type of pressure-sensitive device that emits a greater current of electricity as the amount of applied pressure is increased. Pressure transducers are used in robotics as obstacle and weight sensors.

primary storage unit
The main memory unit of a digital computer, usually consisting of a high-speed direct access unit with moderate storage capacity.

primitive
A pre-programmed basic shape available to the user of a computer graphics program which, when combined with other primitives from the program, can be

used to construct a more complicated composite image. Typical primitives in a two-dimensional computer graphics system are rectangles, circles, ellipses, and lines. Typical primitives in a three-dimensional computer graphics system are boxes, spheres, ellipsoids, and cones.

printed circuit board
An insulating board onto which a circuit has been printed or etched.

printer
An output device which converts electronic signals from a computer into a permanent form readable by humans called hard copy by printing the information onto paper.

printout
Computer output printed on paper.

procedure
A computer program or subroutine.

procedure declaration
See DECLARATION, PROCEDURE.

process bound
A program or system that spends most of its execution time in calculations and operations rather than input or output procedures.

processor
A microprocessor or central processor.

program
A set of instructions the system follows in order to carry out certain tasks.

program counter
The program counter or instruction counter is a register in the CPU (central processing unit), which contains the address of the instruction currently being executed.

program flowchart
A flowchart describing a single project written by a programmer. Program flowcharts are written before the actual program is written and serve as a means of communication between programmers working on the project.

program verification
The task of proving that a given program works correctly.

programmable function keyboard
A button keyboard commonly used with graphics systems to provide input selection for graphics commands.

programming language
A way of communicating with a computer that is much easier than writing programs in machine language binary code. FORTRAN, COBOL, BASIC, and PASCAL are examples.

programming specifications
A document detailing the precise programming steps that must be taken to create a given application.

PROM
An acronym for Programmable Read-Only Memory, which is a computer memory that can be programmed once, but not reprogrammed or adapted.

protecting ring
A plastic ring that strengthens a disk's centre spindle hole. Protection rings are now built into most floppy disks to prolong disk life.

protocol
A relationship between modules in different workstations which define the rules and formats for the exchange of messages.

pseudocode
An imitation of actual computer instructions. Instead of using symbols to describe the programming logic steps, as in flowcharting, pseudocode uses a structure that resembles computer instructions.

pull
See POP.

push
To put an item onto the top of a stack. When an item is inserted at the top of the stack it can be thought of as pushing the other items down one position.

Q

quad density
A technique that records four times as much binary information per unit area of a storage medium as compared to the standard density for that particular medium. Quad density usually applies to floppy disks.

quantize
See DIGITIZE.

quantizer
See DIGITIZER.

queue
A list of items in which additions are made at one end of the list and deletions are made at the other. A queue is like a waiting line – first come, first served. Queues are also called First-In-First-Out or FIFO lists.

quiescent
Refers to an inactive circuit or system. A quiescent circuit is one which at the time is not experiencing an input signal. A quiescent computer system is a system that is either inactive and waiting for input, or a mainframe system whose activity has ceased by not allowing the input of new jobs.

R

radix
The base of a number system. Binary numbers have a radix of 2, and decimal numbers have a radix of 10.

radix point
A character, usually a full point, that separates the integer portion of a number from the fractional portion. For example, the decimal numbers 8.93, 63.45, and 1008.56 all have a radix point.

Random Access Memory (RAM)
A memory device whereby any location in memory can be found, on average, as quickly as any other location. Computer internal memories and disk memories are random access memories. Data is usually stored in bytes, and the RAM storage capacity is measured in kilobytes.

random scan graphics
A video display system in which the cathode ray tube traces out the individual screen images in a series of random lines.

range
A variable's range consists of those values the variable can assume. The range runs from the lowest possible value the variable can assume to the highest possible value it can assume. If, during the execution

of a program, a variable is assigned a number not within its range, a value range error will occur.

raster
A term used in computer graphics to refer to a display image consisting of a matrix of pixels arranged in rows and columns.

raster scan
The horizontal scanning pattern of the electron gun in television sets and computer monitors that use cathode ray tube display.

raster scan graphics
A video display system in which the screen is composed of a set of horizontal lines. The screen is then drawn one row at a time, from the top of the screen down. Raster scan is the display system used in TV and many kinds of computer graphics.

rate joystick
See JOYSTICK, RATE.

rated throughput
Rated throughput is the maximum possible throughput of a data-processing device. Rated throughput is contrasted with effective throughput.

raw data
Data which has not been processed.

read head
A magnetic device which reads data from the storage medium (usually disk or tape).

reader
A device capable of transcribing data from an input medium.

Read-Only Memory (ROM)
Type of computer memory which contains computer instructions that do not need to be changed, such as the instructions for calculating arithmetic functions. The computer can read instructions out of ROM, but no data can be deleted from it or added to it.

readout
Processed information presented to the user, such as on a visual display, line printers, or plotter.

read/write head
A magnetic device which can read from or write onto a storage medium.

real memory
A computer's actual memory that is directly addressable by the central processing unit (CPU).

real time
An application in which the computer response is received immediately, so a user can make a decision at the time the results are received.

real-time processing
A mode of processing data in which the computer is updated almost instantaneously rather than after the next batch of work is processed.

recognizer
A program that determines whether a particular program is valid according to the rules of the specified language.

record
A collection of related data items. A group of records is called a file.

record gap
An area in a storage medium devoid of information that indicates the beginning and end of a physical record. On tape, the record gap delimits records and allows the tape to stop and start between records without losing data.

record length
A measure of the size of a record usually specified in units such as words, bytes, or characters.

recording density
The number of bits in a single linear track measured per unit of length of the recording medium. For example, the recording density of magnetic tape is measured in bits per inch (bpi).

recoverable error
A recoverable error is either an error which can be

corrected or one that does not result in a program's execution terminating abnormally. For example, a rounding error is a recoverable error.

recovery
The process by which a system resumes processing, without irreparable loss of the data in the system, after an error in a program or a malfunction in the equipment has occurred.

rectifier
A circuit that converts alternating current into direct current.

recursion
The process whereby a computer procedure or routine calls itself into operation while being executed or calls another procedure which in turn recalls the original.

re-entry point
The address of the first instruction in the main program to be executed after a subroutine has been completed.

reference count technique
A technique used to reclaim unused storage space. In this method unused cells are reclaimed the instant they become inaccessible to the main program.

refresh
The process whereby an image on a video display

monitor is redrawn periodically by the monitor to stop the image disappearing or noticeable fading.

refresh buffer
A temporary storage location which holds the screen display information as a screen image is refreshed.

refresh memory
A high speed storage unit used in CRT display systems to regenerate the picture being displayed.

refresh rate
The number of times per second an image on the CRT must be redrawn to keep it from flickering.

register
A row of flip-flops used to store a group of binary digits while the computer is processing them.

rehashing
A process undergone when a hash table becomes full. By removing all entries in the original hash table, one by one, and inserting them into a new, larger table, using a new hash function, rehashing creates room for additional entries.

reiteration
See ITERATION.

relational operator
An operator that compares the values of two data items, for example < (less than) and > (greater than).

relativization
A technique which assigns relative addresses to the next written instruction address and operand address. During execution of the program, the relative address is automatically translated to an absolute address.

REM
A key word in BASIC which is used to signify the beginning of a comment.

remote data concentrator
A device which accepts messages from many terminals through slow-speed lines and transmits data to the host processor through a single high-speed synchronous line. This process helps reduce line costs and smoothes out communications to the host processor.

remote station
Data terminal equipment used to communicate with a data processing system from a location that is spatially, temporally, or electrically distant.

resident
A program permanently stored in the computer's main memory or in a certain storage device.

resident program
A program that resides permanently in the storage unit of the central processing unit (CPU).

resistance
A measure of how difficult it is for electric current to flow through a component.

resistor
An electronic component with a fixed amount of resistance to the flow of electric current.

resolution
Refers to the number of pixels or addressable picture elements on the screen. Screen resolution determines the quality of the image on the screen.

resource
Any of the facilities of a computer system that a job or task requires.

resource allocation
To set aside or reserve computer resources for specific jobs or tasks. Resource allocation is one of the primary functions of an operating system.

resource sharing
The simultaneous use of computer facilities by many users.

response time
The time taken by the computer system to respond to the user's commands.

retrieval
The process by which a requested data item is located

in a file and displayed on the terminal from which the request for the data was made.

retrieval, information
The methods and procedures for recovering specific information from stored data. See also RETRIEVAL, MESSAGE.

retrieval, message
The recall of messages some time after the messages have been handled by a message-switching system.

return, carriage
In a character printer, the operation that causes the next character to be printed at the left margin.

return key
See ENTER

reverse video
Dark characters displayed on a light background of a screen. Reverse video is analogous to books, where black-inked characters are printed on white pages.

RGB monitor
Abbreviation for red/green/blue monitor. The type of CRT screen that produces colour images using a trio of red, green, and blue electron guns.

ribbon switch
In the science of robotics, a type of pressure transducer in the form of a long, ribbon-like wire that converts continuous pressure into electricity. Rib-

bon switches can be wrapped around the base of a robot for obstacle detection, or attached to its hands to detect both pressure and weight.

right-justify
To move the contents within a register so that the least significant digit is placed in the rightmost position.

ring network
A network in which terminals and computers are linked together in a circular pattern with each being connected to the two closest to it, one on each side, in the circle.

robotics
The field of artificial intelligence concerned with the design, production, and use of robots.

rotational delay
The time required when accessing a disk for a selected record to pass under the read/write head.

round
To delete one or more least significant figures from a floating point number in order that it be expressed with the limited number of bits that can be represented on the computer.

rounding error
A rounding error occurs when a number is rounded off. For example, if the number 18.9817 is rounded off to 18.98, then the rounding error is .0017.

route, alternative

A secondary communication path used to reach a destination if the main route is unavailable.

row

A horizontal arrangement of characters, bits, or other expressions. Contrasts with column.

RPG

Abbreviation for Report Program Generator. A business-orientated programming language.

RUN

A statement in BASIC which causes execution of the currently stored program to begin.

run-time

The period of time a program spends actually being executed by a computer.

run-time error

An error that occurs during the execution of a program causing the execution to terminate abnormally.

S

scalar

A scalar quantity has magnitude but no direction in space. For example, temperature is scalar but velocity is not.

scan
To examine sequentially part by part.

scatter-read
Refers to placing information from a physical record into nonadjacent locations in memory. Opposite of gather-write.

scrolling
An operation that virtually all computer operating systems use to display data and keyboard input on the screen. Input and output appear at the bottom of the screen and travel upwards as more lines are written at the bottom. When a message reaches the top of the screen, it disappears to continue allowing more messages to be written at the bottom.

second generation computer
Describes computers produced between about 1959 and 1964, the second era of computer technology development, in which the transistor replaced the vacuum tube.

secondary storage device
A device which provides additional memory for a computer system. The memory in secondary storage is usually non-volatile. In other words, is not affected if the computer is turned off or being used to execute another program. Examples of secondary storage devices are magnetic tape units and disk storage units.

secure kernel
A well-defined segment of the system software which is carefully protected by specific, often elaborate, access controls.

seek time
The measurement of the time it requires for a disk drive's read/write head to find a specific track. A drive's seek time is one factor by which its overall speed is determined.

segment *(noun)*
A record containing one or more data items. Segments are the basic divisions of data passing to and from application programs under control of database management software.

segment *(verb)*
To divide a computer program into parts so that the program can be executed without the entire program being in internal storage at any one time.

selective clock stretching
A technique capable of resolving digital timing differences among system components and obtaining the maximum performance out of each component.

semiconductor
A material, such as silicon, that is neither a good conductor nor a good insulator. Semiconductor devices, such as diodes, transistors, and integrated

circuits, are the essential parts in modern computer systems.

send-only device
A device, such as a terminal, which can send data to the computer but cannot receive data from it.

sense
An attempt to detect holes or marks in or on storage media.

sequential access device
A memory device, such as magnetic tape, in which data items can be reached only in sequence.

sequential file
A data file whose records are stored sequentially. Each record is written immediately after the previous record. This is perhaps the most straightforward method of file organization. Because sequential files are stored sequentially, they use less memory space per byte of usable data than any other method of file organization. However, the average retrieval time of a particular record is slow, since the computer must search each record, starting from the beginning, until it finds the desired record. Similarly, the average time to store a record is slow since the computer must search each record to the end of the file in order to determine where the next record will be written.

serial-access memory

A memory device in which, in order to find the desired item, all the items which occur before it must be read first.

servomechanism

A device to monitor an operation as it proceeds and to make necessary adjustments to keep the operation under control.

set, character

The numbers, letters, and symbols associated with a given device or coding system.

shadow mask CRT

A type of CRT used in colour monitors and colour TV sets, in which a screen, the shadow mask, is used to align the phosphor dots on the screen with their respective electron guns.

shannon

A choice between two equally probable events.

shared memory

A memory chip (usually RAM) that can be accessed by two different CPUs. This allows the CPUs to use the same data and communicate with each other. Shared memory chips are also called dual-port memory chips.

shift, phase

A change in time relationship of one part of a signal waveform with another, with no change in the basic form of the signal. The degree of change varies with frequency as a signal passes through a channel.

shift register
A register in which all the bits can be moved one place to the left (or the right) when a particular control signal is pulsed.

side effect
This occurs when operations performed in one section of a program have an unintended effect on another section of the program.

signal-to-noise ratio
The ratio of the power in the transmitted signal to the undesirable noise present in the absence of any signal.

silicon
The main material used to make semiconductors.

silicon chip
A small piece of silicon on which very complex miniaturized circuits are made by photographic and chemical processes. Silicon chips are semiconductors.

simplex channel
A communications channel that allows transmissions in one direction only.

simplex transmission
Mode of transmission used for communication which

is capable of transmitting data only in one direction. Simplex lines are designed such that one end contains only a transmitter and the other end contains only a receiver.

simulation
The process of representing one system by another; for instance, representing the real world by a mathematical model solved by a computer.

simulator
A device or a program that mathematically simulates a certain system or process in order to enable people to study it.

single address
See ADDRESS, SINGLE.

skew
A degree of nonsynchronization in supposedly parallel elements.

skip
To ignore one or more instructions in a sequence of instructions.

slab
A small group of binary digits.

slave
A device that operates under the control of another device.

slewing rate
The rate at which blank paper can be physically moved through the printer or the rate that output can be driven over the allowable range.

smooth
To apply procedures to a sequential set of numerical data items in a manner designed to reduce or eliminate rapid fluctuations in data which are referred to as noise or 'data errors'.

soft copy
A copy of a computer's output which appears on the screen of a visual display device. Soft copies, unlike hard copies, cannot be carried away from the computer by a user. Soft copy can also refer to output in audio format or in any other form that is not hard copy.

software
All the programs, computer languages, and operations used to make a computer perform a useful function. Software contrasts with hardware which constitutes all the tangible, physical elements of a computer system such as printers and CPUs.

software configuration
The types of, and relationships between, the system control programs installed in a computer system. These control programs include operating systems, assemblers, and compilers.

software engineers
A specialized group of programmers who work for computer manufacturers and usually create the systems software that operates the equipment for the user.

software tool
A program that is used to help solve a data-processing problem. Software tools are often used as aids in writing programs for more complicated applications.

software-compatible
Two or more computers are software-compatible if they use the same machine language, and, therefore, can execute the same programs. For example, all Atari 800 computers are software-compatible. Similarly, all Apple II computers are software-compatible.

solid state
Describes a device whose operation depends on the bulk properties of the solid materials of which it is made, as opposed to devices such as vacuum and gas tubes.

solid-state cartridge
A plug-in ROM module that is used on many small computers. Each module contains a preprogrammed function.

SOM
Abbreviation for Start Of Message.

sort *(noun)*
A processing operation that distributes information in alphabetical, numerical, or alphanumerical groups according to a given rule.

sort *(verb)*
To arrange a set of items in a particular order.

sort field
A specified field in a record used to sort the records of a file.

sorting network
A device used for sorting data. In these networks, data is inputted into the network in an 'unordered' spatial relationship and output from the network sorted into a specific spatial order.

source program
A program written in a high-level programming language (such as BASIC) which must be translated into machine language before it can be executed by the computer.

space
A capacity for storing data, as on a disk, tape or in main memory.

special symbol
A special symbol is a character that is neither a letter nor a number. For example, # and £ are both special symbols.

spinwriter
A type of high-quality computer printer.

split screen
A display device screen capable of displaying part of a file on one part of the screen and another part of the same or a different file on another part of the screen.

spooling
A technique by which data is moved from a slow input/output (I/O) device (e.g. card reader) to a fast input/output device (e.g. magnetic disk) before that data is accessed by main storage or output for the user. This helps to minimize the speed disparity between the internal speeds of the computer and the input/output devices.

spreadsheet
A popular type of financial modelling package of which VisiCalc is an example.

sprite
A user-defined block of pixels that can be placed anywhere on the screen. Sprites are maintained directly by the hardware and simplify the programming of video games.

stack
A list of items with additions and deletions made to the list at one end – the top of the stack. Stacks are called Last-In-First-Out or LIFO lists. A stack is comparable to a stack of plates in a cafeteria where

adding a plate pushes the rest down and removing a plate pops the rest up.

stack register
A special register within the central processing unit (CPU) which keeps track of return addresses for subroutine jumps. The stack is a Last-In-First-Out structure that is able to retain the correct return addresses for subroutines.

stacked job processing
A technique that permits multiple jobs to be stacked for presentation to the system which automatically processes the jobs one after the other.

start bit
A bit used in asynchronous transmission to signal the beginning of transmission of a group of data bits, such as a character. Start bits enable the receiver to tell where a new group of data starts.

start/stop drives
Start/stop drives pause in inter-record gaps on the tape surface as they read or write data.

statement
A set of instructions that make up one unit of a computer program.

station
1 An input or output point on a communication system; a terminal; a machine. **2** A telephone set. **3** A magnetic tape unit.

stop bit

A bit used in asynchronous transmission to signal the end of transmission of a group of data bits, such as those making up a character. Having a stop bit at the end of each group of data bits improves readability.

storage

A device to which data can be transferred and from which it can be obtained at a later time.

storage capacity

Storage capacity, or 'capacity', refers to the amount of information a computer system or storage device (tape, disk and so on) is capable of storing at any one time. A personal computer with a capacity of 64K will be able to store 65,536 bytes of information in its inbuilt memory.

storage protection

Protection against unauthorized writing in and/or reading from all or part of a storage device by means of codes, special programming, or instructions.

store

To transmit the data from the central processing unit (CPU) or an input device to a computer memory device.

stored program

Instructions are kept in a computer's internal memory for execution in the same form that data is kept. A program can be designed to alter itself as required when stored in this way.

stored program computer
A computer that can store its own instructions as well as data.

string
A group of characters stored in a computer.

stroke analysis
A method used to identify characters by dissecting them into prescribed elements. The sequence, relative positions, and number of detected elements are then used to determine the specific character.

structured design
An approach to problem solving using a set of guidelines, techniques and special symbols to determine a set of interconnected modules or procedures, organized in a hierarchical fashion that will resolve a certain problem.

structured programming
Refers to the process of writing programs that are easy to understand because they have well-defined structures.

STX
Abbreviation for Start-of-Text. It is a control character that designates the boundary between the message heading and the text of a message to be

transmitted. In ASCII, the STX character is represented by the ASCII code '002'.

sublist
A sublist is a list within a larger list. For example, within the list (a,b,c,(aa,bb),(dd,ee,ff)) (aa,bb) and (dd,ee,ff) are both sublists.

subprogram
A segment of a program which performs a specific function. If that function is to be carried out more than once, a subprogram can help reduce the amount of programming required, as the function only needs to be programmed once and can be executed as required during the program.

subroutine
A set of instructions given a particular name that will be executed when a main program calls for it.

subroutine library
A collection of subroutines that can be used in conjunction with various routines with little or no modification.

subscript
A symbol or number that is used to identify an element in an array.

subscripted array
See INDEXED ARRAY.

subscripted list
See INDEXED ARRAY.

supervisor
The part of the control program of the operating system that coordinates the use of resources and maintains the flow of operations for the central processing unit of the computer.

supervisory routine
The control routine that initiates and directs all other programs and routines.

suppress
To eliminate zeros or other insignificant characters from a computer printout.

surge
A sudden, usually undesirable, voltage or current change in an operating circuit. Surges are generally caused by a shorted circuit component or the collapse of a magnetic field.

switch
1 To establish a temporary interconnection between two or more stations over communications paths. **2** A short term for a line or message switcher.

switch register
The most basic microprocessor input device, which is simply a row of switches. Each switch corresponds to a single bit in the microprocessor data word. When the user wishes to enter information into the

microprocessor, the switches are set up for a logic 1
and down for a logic 0.

switching centre
In data communications, a device which routes data
from incoming circuits to the proper outgoing
circuits.

synchronizer
A storage device used to compensate for a difference
in a rate of flow of information or time of occurrence
of events when transmitting information from one
device to another.

synchronous
Describes events occurring in regular, timed intervals kept continuously in step with an electronic
clocking device.

synchronous circuit
A circuit whose operation is controlled by a
synchronizing clock pulse.

synchronous transmission
Technique by which data is transmitted at regular,
timed intervals, from one location to another.

syntax
The set of rules in a programming language that
specify how the language symbols can be put
together to form meaningful statements. Syntax
rules are like grammar rules.

syntax checker
A computer program that tests source statements in a programming language to detect violations of the syntax or rules of structure of that language.

syntax error
A programming error in the structure, or syntax, of an instruction or set of instructions. All syntax errors in a compiled program must be corrected before the program can be executed. In an interpreted program, only those syntax errors pertaining to individual instructions must be corrected before the program can be executed. During execution, syntax errors in groups of instructions, such as loops and subroutines, can then be detected.

system
Group of interrelated devices and elements which can function together. In computer systems the central processing unit (CPU) controls the other elements.

system design
The specification of the working relations between all the parts of a system in terms of their characteristic actions.

system catalog (SYSCTLG)
A computer system's file that serves as an index to all other files that the system has used or will use. The SYSCTLG shows the names, sizes, locations, and

usually any other pertinent information about the files.

system diagnostics
A program used to detect overall system malfunctions.

systems program
A program, supplied by the computer vendor, that enables the user to use the computer more easily and more effectively. A collection of these programs forms the computer's operating system.

systems programmer
A person who plans, generates, maintains, extends and controls the use of an operating system to improve overall productivity of the installation.

systems analyst
A person who defines a problem in data processing terms and may indicate to programmers the directions for specific data processing solutions.

systems flowchart
A flowchart which describes a computer system and which is written and used by systems analysts.

systems software
The software which comes with the machine, from the manufacturer, and is the general name for the set of programs that make the machine run itself effectively.

T

tablet
An input device used with interactive graphics to locate a place on the screen. The tablet is used with a stylus or hand cursor which locates screen position.

tape
A ribbon of flexible material used as a storage medium, described by a qualifying adjective such as paper, magnetic, oiled, and so on. The word 'tape' is most commonly used to refer to magnetic tape.

tape drive
A device that converts information stored on magnetic tape into signals that can be sent to a computer, and that receives information from the computer and stores it on magnetic tape.

tape label
An identifying label on the first record of a magnetic tape.

target market
The target market is the market (industrial or private) for which computer hardware or software is specifically designed.

technical writer
A technical writer is a person who writes technical documentation professionally.

telecommunications
The transmission of data over a distance, usually by electrical means. Contrasts with directly-connected equipment in close proximity.

telegraphy
A system of communication for the transmission of graphic symbols, usually letters or numerals, by use of a signal code. Now includes the use of teletypewriters.

telemetry
Transmission of data over great distances, especially remote control of apparatus and equipment.

teleprocessing
The use of telecommunications systems by a computer which involves data acquisition, message switching, and computer-to-computer or computer-to-terminal communications.

TELEX
An international communications service which uses teleprinters.

template
A plastic card with flowchart symbols cut out of it.

terminal
1 A point in a system or communication network at which data can either enter or leave. 2 An input-output device capable of transmitting entries to and obtaining output from the system of which it is a part.

test file
A file of data that is used to check a computer program for errors during its development. Sometimes called a 'program test file' or 'program test data'.

testing
The process of running the computer program and evaluating the program results, in order to determine if any errors exist.

test run
A test run is the execution of a program using test data in order to determine whether or not logical errors or syntactical errors exist in the program.

text
The part of a message that contains the main body of information to be conveyed.

text editor
A program that facilitates changes to computer-stored information; assists in the preparation of text.

thermal printer
A dot-matrix printer that forms characters by pressing hot wires onto special paper. A thermal printer does not use ink or ribbons.

thermionic emission
Thermionic emission occurs where a heated metal surface gives off electrons. It is by thermionic emission that the electron gun in a CRT gives off electrons which illuminate the screen-surface.

thimble printer

One of seven main types of impact printer. Thimble printers produce fully formed characters by pressing a print element, shaped like a thimble, against an inked ribbon and paper. The thimble contains two rows of characters and rotates and tips up and down to print the characters required.

thin film

An electronic component coated with molecular deposits of material in specially designed patterns.

third generation

Describes computers produced beginning 1964, the third era of computer technology development in which integrated circuitry and miniaturization replaced transistors.

thrashing

In a virtual storage environment, thrashing refers to an excessive amount of moving pages from secondary storage to the internal storage.

throughput

1 The rate at which information can be accurately delivered when averaged over a long period of time.
2 The time required to perform an operation from the time it begins until the time it is successfully completed.

throughput time
The time required for work to be processed by the personnel and equipment in computer operations.

time sharing
A time-sharing computer system allows several users to be connected simultaneously to the same computer.

time slice
A uniform interval of CPU time allocated for use in performing a task.

time slicing
Breaking the CPU time into a series of brief periods, or 'slices', each allocated to different programs in turn, to prevent the monopolization of the CPU by any one program.

time, turnaround
1 The time taken to 'turn round' a processing job ie the time between submission of the job and its completion. **2** The time required to reverse the echo-suppressors on a switched telephone circuit. **3** The time required for a system to transfer from the receive mode to the transmit mode, or vice versa.

tone
The audible result of a frequency within the audio range (approximately 20 to 20,000 Hz).

total, batch
See TOTAL, HASH.

total, hash

A sum formed for error-checking purposes by adding fields that are not normally related by unit of measure, eg, a total of invoice serial numbers.

touch panel

A touch-sensitive screen that is mounted onto the face of a CRT. Allows users to input a choice of options to the computer by simply touching a location on the screen.

TPI

Abbreviation for Tracks Per Inch. There are 48TPI in a 5¼" floppy with 40 tracks used for actual data storage. High density floppies have 96 TPI with 80 tracks for actual storage.

track

Information is stored on a magnetic disk in one of a number of concentric circles, each of which is called a track.

trackball

A device used with interactive graphics to control cursor position on the screen. Trackballs are used as cursor locators in computer aided design and arcade games.

Tracks Per Inch

See TPI

transceiver
A device that both transmits and receives data, often simultaneously.

transducer
A special device used to convert energy from one form to another. For example, quartz embedded in mercury can act as a transducer and can change electric energy to sound energy.

transistor
An electronic device utilizing semiconductor properties to control the flow of currents.

translator
A device that converts programs written in one language into programs in another language.

transmission, carrier
Transmission in which the transmitted electric wave results from the modulation of a single-frequency wave by an information-carrying (modulating) wave.

transmitter-start code (TSC)
The unique code sent to a particular teletypewriter on a circuit to cause it to transmit its tape.

trapdoor
A breach created intentionally in an electronic data processing system for the purpose of collecting, altering, or destroying data later.

tree
A connected, acyclic graph. That is, in a tree there are no cycles and there is a path from any node to any other node, resembling a tree.

trivial segmentation
Occurs when an initial segmentation is formed, with each data item stored in a separate segment.

Trojan horse
A computer program that is apparently or actually useful and contains a trapdoor, leading to the execution of an entirely different process.

troubleshoot
To search for and find a malfunction in a hardware unit or a mistake in a computer program.

truncate
To drop all the digits of a number that are to the right of the decimal point.

trunk
A circuit between two telephone exchanges or switching centres, or from an exchange to a customer's switchboard.

tunnel diode
An electronic device with switching speeds of fractional billionths of seconds.

turnaround time
See TIME, TURNAROUND

turnkey
Refers to a computer system sold complete and ready to use for a specific application; requires no additional hardware modification or planning.

two-sided disk status
Signals the system whenever a double side disk is installed.

type bar
Contains all of the characters in a certain character set. Type bars are used for printing. Different type bars can contain different character sets and can be used interchangeably.

type, channel
Simplex, half-duplex, and duplex circuits are channel types. The names indicate only the directional capability of the channel.

U

unary
A logical operation that requires only one input value. The negation, or NOT operation, is an example of a unary operation. Unary is synonymous with monadic, and contrasted with binary or dyadic.

unconditional branch
A branch which is always executed. There is no

condition that must be satisfied for the branch to occur.

unit
1 A basic element. **2** A device having a special function.

unit, central processing
See CENTRAL PROCESSING UNIT.

Unix
A machine-independent operating system developed by the American electronics giant AT&T.

unpack
To take a packed unit of storage and break it down into its individual components.

unsigned integer
An unsigned integer is an integer value with neither a positive (+) nor a negative (-) sign. Unsigned integers are assumed to be positive. For example, 18 and 36 are both unsigned integers.

unsigned real number
An unsigned real number is a real number with neither a positive (+) nor a negative (-) sign. Unsigned real numbers, such as 16.32 and 45.936, are assumed to be positive.

up
A computer system is up when it is available for use.

update
To change the data in a file or record to incorporate new or more current information.

up-line loading
See UPLOAD.

upload
To transfer a copy of a program, file, or other information from the user's own terminal to a remote database or other computer over a communications line. Upload is synonymous with up-line loading.

uptime
The period of time during which a computer system is up, or operating correctly.

user
A person who uses a computer.

user area (UA)
Area on a magnetic disk for storing semi-permanent data such as programs, subprograms, and subroutines. In contrast, reserved areas are used for storing things that may not be written into, such as compilers and track and sector information.

user-friendly
Implies a computing system that provides for the capabilities and limitations of the operator. A user-friendly system is easy to use and understand for a wide variety of people, rather than forcing the user to become expert in the technicalities of computing.

utility program
A program in general support of a computer, for example, a monitoring routine.

V

vacuum tube
An electronic component consisting of electrodes placed inside an evacuated glass tube.

valence electron
An electron that is only loosely connected to its atom; hence it can be dislodged easily.

validation
The testing of data to see if it correctly adheres to a designated criterion, such as prescribed limits or specified order.

variable
A variable is a symbolic name representing a value that changes during the program's execution.

variable-length record
A data record whose length is not fixed to any constant value. The actual length of a particular record is attached to the front of the record's data so that the program can recognize a record's length.

VDU
See VISUAL DISPLAY UNIT.

vector
A quantity is a vector if it has both magnitude and direction in space. For example, velocity is a vector while temperature is not.

vector data aggregate
A vector data aggregate is one type of data aggregate. For example, a vector data aggregate called DATE is composed of data items called MONTH, DAY and YEAR.

vector-graphics display
A display system in which the electron beam 'paints' the desired image on the display screen. Unlike raster-scan displays, vector-graphics displays do not scan horizontal lines to create images.

vendor
A company that sells computers, peripheral devices, or computer services.

verb
An instruction in a programming language that causes action. For example, READ, WRITE, and PRINT are all verbs.

verifier
A device on which a record can be compared or tested for identity character-by-character with a copy as it is being prepared.

vertical redundancy check (VRC)
An error-checking method whereby parity bits are used for each character.

vertical tab
A machine function that causes the print mechanism or cursor to move to a specific line while staying in the same column.

video terminal
A device for entering information into and receiving information from a computer system and displaying it on a screen. A typewriter-like keyboard is used to enter information.

videodisc
Direct access device used for storing audio and visual information to be replayed on a television screen. Videodiscs are analogous to magnetic disks for computers.

videotex
Any of the various systems which make computer-based information available through VDUs and modified TV sets to people at home and at work.

virtual storage
A technique to maximize and optimize the storage available in a computer by using areas on secondary storage devices as extensions of internal storage. Pages of data are swapped back and forth from disk to storage unit as required.

VisiCalc
The brand name of a software package used for financial planning and budgeting. The success of VisiCalc led to a number of similar products being launched.

visual display unit (VDU)
A peripheral device that displays information on a television-like screen. An example of a visual display unit is a CRT. Visual display units usually have an attached keyboard used for entering data.

Voice Answer Back (VAB)
An audio response device that can link a computer system to a telephone network to provide voice responses to inquiries made from telephone-tape terminals.

voice grade channel
A channel that permits transmission of speech and accommodates frequencies from 300 to 3000Hz. Also suitable for the transmission of digital or analog data.

voice recognition
An interface technology in which human voice patterns are analyzed by a machine to determine words spoken. Recognized commands are sent to a computer system that converts them into physical functions.

volt
Unit of measure of electric potential.

volume
Removable mass storage unit such as a magnetic reel of tape or a disk pack containing documents and a directory identifying its contents.

volume table of contents (VTOC)
A file containing the names, sizes, locations, and other pertinent information about all the files contained on a large, fixed disk. On small floppy disks, the VTOC is usually called the directory.

W

wand
An input device used to read optical bar code labels by sensing the optical pattern of the light and dark areas.

warmstart
A way of resetting a computer without erasing the contents of memory. The program in memory is preserved, and only elements of the operating system are reset.

Winchester disk
A popular type of fixed disk used with microcomputer systems.

window
A rectangular region of the screen which can display its own graphics image, independent of the rest of the screen's display.

wire
A string of conducting material (such as copper) set up so that electrical current can flow between two points.

wire-matrix printer
An impact printer which prints dot-matrix characters, one at a time, by pressing the ends of certain wires against an inked ribbon and paper.

word
A string of bits which can occupy a single addressable location. A word is interpreted by different processors of the computer as different items, such as instructions, quantities, and alphanumeric characters.

word length
The number of bits making up a word. The word length may either be a fixed or a variable number of bits.

word processor
A computer-based system or software package which allows the user to input text to the system which can then be edited or reformatted at will before being printed out.

word wrap
Describes how a program reformats text in a word processing system after insertions or deletions. Without it, a user can spend more time reformatting than inserting and deleting. In automatic word wrap, a program reformats a paragraph each time editing extends or shortens a line, so that text always appears neatly positioned.

Wordstar
The brand name of a popular software package used for word processing.

workfile
A temporary working copy of the program currently being edited.

write
The process of transferring data from a computer to an output device.

write head
A magnetic device used to write data on a storage medium, such as a magnetic tape or disk.

write-protect disable
Overrides the physical write-protect tab on a disk, letting a software manufacturer write software to write-protected disks without inserting or removing tabs.

write-protect tab
A notch on one or both sides of floppy and

microfloppy disks that can be covered by an adhesive tab to prevent new data from being written on that side of the disk, thereby protecting existing data.

X

XMT
Abbreviation for transmit.

XMTR
Abbreviation for transmitter.

Z

zap
To erase.

zero compression
The process which eliminates the storage of insignificant leading zeros, and these are to the left of the most significant digits.

zero condition
The state of a magnetic cell when it represents zero.

zero fill
A type of filling or padding in which the unused portion of a field, record, or fixed-length data block is padded with zeros. For example, if a numeric field is 8 digits long, and the number 714 is inserted into it,

the zero fill routine would pad the leading portion with zeros, after which it would read 00000714.

zero suppression
An editing operation designed to convert computable numerals into human-readable format.

zerodivide
An error condition which occurs when a program reaches an operation that requires it to divide by zero. Normally the program will stop and an error message will be printed.